AF623514

HOW

some small businesses get their ducks in a row and

GROW

While others remain undistinguished

■

Shil Niyogi

SAGE | Response Business Books
www.sagepublications.com
Los Angeles • London • New Delhi • Singapore • Washington DC

Copyright © Shil Niyogi, 2012

All rights reserved. No part of this book may be reproduced or utilized in any form or by any means, electronic or mechanical, including photocopying, recording or by any information storage or retrieval system, without permission in writing from the publisher.

First published in 2012 by

SAGE Response
B1/I-1 Mohan Cooperative Industrial Area
Mathura Road, New Delhi 110 044, India

SAGE Publications Inc
2455 Teller Road
Thousand Oaks, California 91320, USA

SAGE Publications Ltd
1 Oliver's Yard
55 City Road
London EC1Y 1SP, United Kingdom

SAGE Publications Asia-Pacific Pte Ltd
33 Pekin Street
#02-01 Far East Square
Singapore 048763

Published by Vivek Mehra for SAGE Publications India Pvt Ltd, typeset in 12/14 Adobe Garamond by Star Compugraphics Private Limited, Delhi and printed at Chaman Enterprises, New Delhi.

Library of Congress Cataloging-in-Publication Data

Niyogi, Shil.

How some small businesses get their ducks in a row and grow while others remain undistinguished/Shil Niyogi.

p. cm.

Includes bibliographical references.

1. Organizational effectiveness. 2. Management—Social aspects. 3. Entrepreneurship. I. Title.

HD58.9.N59 658.02'2—dc23 2011 2011042899

ISBN: 987-81-321-0753-8 (PB)

The SAGE Team: Sachin Sharma, Arpita Dasgupta, Rajib Chatterjee and Rajinder Kaur

Contents

Thank you for choosing a SAGE product! If you have any comment, observation or feedback, I would like to personally hear from you. Please write to me at contactceo@sagepub.in

—Vivek Mehra, Managing Director and CEO,
SAGE Publications India Pvt Ltd, New Delhi

Bulk Sales

SAGE India offers special discounts for purchase of books in bulk. We also make available special imprints and excerpts from our books on demand.

For orders and enquiries, write to us at

Marketing Department
SAGE Publications India Pvt Ltd
B1/I-1, Mohan Cooperative Industrial Area
Mathura Road, Post Bag 7
New Delhi 110044, India
E-mail us at marketing@sagepub.in

Get to know more about SAGE, be invited to SAGE events, get on our mailing list. Write today to marketing@sagepub.in

This book is also available as an e-book.

Preface

WHAT do Jack Welch (GE), Howard Schultz (Starbucks), and Ray Kroc (McDonalds) have in common that made their firms grow beyond excellence? Their vision, their leadership styles, their people management skills, or their industry insight? Perhaps one factor that leads them all is their talent for executing successful turnarounds. Almost all of us have come across growth catalysts and turnaround agents, who have helped entrepreneurs and small businesses grow. And entrepreneurs form a vital component of the global and the national economies. Supporting the importance of entrepreneurs, Vinod Khosla (the founding CEO of Sun Microsystems) points out that entrepreneurs drive technology and are responsible for approximately 40 percent of America's GDP growth.[1] Hence, it has become imperative for entrepreneurship to thrive. As this book goes to press, all the nations are looking for emerging technologies and entrepreneurs to turn around what could be a global recession of enormous magnitude. *This book will serve these entrepreneurs in reassessing their options and planning their effectual moves.*

With the changing economy and a subsequent reduction in headcounts in larger and mid-size firms, the workforce also has to shift to smaller businesses and entrepreneurs. According to a survey conducted by Michigan State University's Collegiate Employment Research Institute, hiring of graduates would spike

15 percent at smaller companies.[2] Due to this increasing trend to seek employment with an entrepreneur, a huge emphasis needs to be put on managing entrepreneurs and their organizations, particularly when these undistinguished (or average) entrepreneurs have their own rules. Rules that are not documented—and certainly not taught anywhere. *This book will be a great exercise in learning to work with such entrepreneurs to sustain and grow their businesses successfully.*

Issues at these entrepreneurial firms come in different shapes and sizes. Designed as a boot-camp–style workbook, this book will assist you in handling issues, examining their root causes, and infusing new energy into the undistinguished entrepreneur's firm, either directly or through turnaround specialists and venture capitalists.

To help engender growth at such undistinguished enterprises, I have divided the book into three broad categories (using my Procedure–Behavior–Strategy Framework) to help you:

- follow the existing norms and introduce better standards and more effective procedures within the firm (***Procedural***),
- attend to the human side of the enterprise and the entrepreneur (***Behavioral***), and finally
- develop long-term plans for the entrepreneur and the enterprise (***Strategic***).

■

Acknowledgments

THE idea of this book has its origin in multiple sources of inspiration, knowledge, and experience.

Much of what I have learned over the years came as the result of my interactions with over a thousand people who work at small businesses. From each one of them, I have learned about entrepreneurship and how small businesses die if the passion of *doing it better* fades away. I am thankful to them.

I am thankful to all the entrepreneurs I have worked with and the faculty who taught me entrepreneurship at the Anderson School of Management, University of California, Los Angeles, USA. I am particularly thankful to Bill Yost, whose entrepreneurial operations class made us think through "what should an entrepreneur do first thing Monday AM," and to Bill Cockrum, whose entrepreneurial finance class made him a top entrepreneurship professor in the US.[3]

I am grateful to some of the world's leading thought leaders, particularly Adrian Slywotzky, Ajay Lavakare, Ajit Rangnekar, Alex Andon, Amitai Etzioni, Chip and Dan Heath, Daniel Goleman, Daniel Kahneman, David Kirsch, David Lewin, Ellie Miller, Eric Flamholtz, Garr Reynolds, Gomatam Venkatesh, Gregory Rose, Guy Kawasaki, Henry Mintzberg, Herbert Woodward, Hibah Yousuf, Howard H. Stevenson, Jack Dangermond, Jeff Wilke, Jeffrey Pfeffer, John O. Whitney, Joseph C. Nunes, Kathy Marshack, Melissa Gould, Michael

J. Roberts, Nitish Kumar, Neil C. Churchill, Noah Goldstein, P.B. Sharma, Phil Gardner, Richard Giorla, Rick Wartzman, Rita McGrath, Robert Ronstadt, Sharon Bernstein, Silvano Arieti, T.J. Rodgers, Uday Karmarkar, Vinod Khosla, and Xavier Drèze for their work, their ideas, and research contributions that helped me immensely while writing this book. I am profoundly obliged to them for sharing their wisdom on making an impact in the entrepreneurial environment and bringing about more control.

I am also thankful to Harvard Business School Publishing for providing me with permission to quote from authors' works. Tad Dearden, from Harvard Business School Publishing may be contacted for information regarding the originals.

I am immensely grateful to Sugata Ghosh and Premendra Sharma of SAGE Publications for their help throughout this project. Thanks are also due to Rekha Natarajan, Arpita Dasgupta, Sachin Sharma, and the entire SAGE team for their constant efforts in improving the book layout and making it more impactful.

The most significant credit goes to my family—to my Dad and Mom, who taught me the importance of life goals and **procedures** to help me in what I do; to my wife for loving me and aligning our individual goals and seeing how I live my life to the fullest—thus influencing my **behavior**; and to my brother for showing me the big picture and helping me rethink and refine my **strategies** from time to time. And also to my parents-in-law for sharing with me some of their entrepreneurial experiences, without which the book would have been incomplete.

■

Introduction

IN my interactions with owners of small businesses, I have noticed that one factor is common to all—they face several roadblocks at the outset. However, those small business owners that have perpetual problems with assessing their goals (where they want to go), misguided perspectives (thinking in the short term as opposed to developing long-term strategies), limited market understanding and vision (lack of knowledge or interest in new technologies, new lines of business, new business designs), poor budget allocation skills (increased spending as opposed to being frugal and reinvesting in the firm growth), a hunger for fame (without any meaningful innovations or breakthroughs), and a highly impulsive and emotional disposition, remain "undistinguished" (*uhn-di-sting-gwisht: adjective. Having no distinguishing marks or features; unnoticed; inconspicuous. Synonyms: mediocre, ordinary, unexceptional, unremarkable*).

Undistinguished entrepreneurs (UEs) never grow until they leave these facets of mediocrity behind. This book is dedicated to them.

This book looks into the numerous areas the employees can focus on to keep themselves out of the day-to-day firefighting with the undistinguished entrepreneur. It will help employees avoid the straining relationships that result from the undistinguished entrepreneur's attitude and practices. Through my observations, I have come up with the most frequently faced issues of such entrepreneurs and ways to handle them so as to make a reliable impression every time.

To help us understand and work toward the undistinguished enterprise's growth, we will be using a Procedure–Behavior–Strategy framework, or, a PBS framework (there was a brief period when I had deliberated over ProBeSt being more memorable and perhaps an apt acronym, but after conducting a short family-survey, which is what I say when I consult my wife, I felt PBS was better). So, I divided the book into three sections. The Procedural section points out ways to define, implement, and follow procedures within the firm. The Behavioral section looks at ways to align oneself with the firm goals, build culture within the firm, and forecast the entrepreneur's behavior for effective decision-making. The Strategic section centers on assessing the company's goals, planning the firm's future, and driving the firm to be a frontrunner in the industry.

It is a natural human tendency to take care of the basic needs or fix existing procedures first, very similar to what Maslow's hierarchy of needs theorizes. If you are without food, water, and sleep, you cannot think of morality, creativity, and achievement. If you do not have money for rent, how can you think of travel (unless it is all paid for)? Similarly, if you do not have the right procedures, how can you make strategic changes?

This is similar to buying a bank-owned home. You need to fix up the place before you start thinking of buying chandeliers. Once you have set an amenable comfort-rendering environment (Procedural), you start living gracefully in it. You want to keep it clean—not throw stuff around, mow the lawn, keep your voices soft and low, and establish good relationships with neighbors. You teach this to your family members as well, thus establishing a culture (Behavioral).

And then you meet an old idea-filled friend (or read a cerebral magazine) and you start thinking of increasing the value of your property by installing a swimming pool or converting an open space into a room. There is a price to pay for all that extra work, but the outcome, as a major credit card commercial would say, is priceless (Strategic).

Another PBS framework example: Ever wondered why the flight attendant in safety demonstrations, instructs us to put on our oxygen masks first, before putting them on our children? It is definitely not because our life is more important than our child's. The idea is to prevent our potential loss of control from cabin decompression and loss of oxygen (hypoxia). When hypoxia sets in, we cannot even get to a mask, let alone to the passenger next to us. So, what we see is a procedural fix (P) when the passenger puts the mask on; a behavioral phase (B) when he or she regains control and can think of the next step; and finally, a strategic move (S) when the passenger takes the mask and puts it on the child.

Take our school system—again, a case of the PBS framework. In the elementary school, you work on your math, science, language, art, among other subjects, to set basic procedures inside you. These subjects and other influences help identify your strengths and orient your behavior. And with that behavior, you choose goals and work toward them strategically. In sum, right procedures, right behavior, and, finally, the right strategy lead you there.

The examples in the book illustrate the common mistakes that we all make while working in entrepreneurial organizations. The sooner we recognize patterns of problems and take control with improved processes, build adaptability, and make strategic endeavors to improve, the faster our entrepreneurial company will grow.

■

Procedural Ways

To help you improve procedures within the entrepreneurial firm and adhere to those

BEFORE Linh Chun started teaching science at a small elementary school in a suburb of Shanghai, she worked as a freelance medical [illegible] at hospitals. It took her 10 years of medical practice and [illegible] of entrepreneurship [illegible] and then [illegible] With time [illegible] pier and he [illegible] When her husband [illegible] Moving into the [illegible] the suburban [illegible] ing from her [illegible] clients [illegible] a strong sales [illegible] school. The [illegible] who had [illegible] Two days after [illegible] a procedure [illegible] back. "What [illegible]"

Rajiv Sinha moved back to India after [illegible] from an American [illegible] he stay close to the family [illegible] the States to take [illegible] a friend of his father's [illegible] pany. With the [illegible] Korean global giant [illegible] efficiency of [illegible]

BEFORE Linh Chun started teaching science at a small elementary school in a suburb of Shanghai, she worked as a freelance medical transcriptionist at hospitals. It took her 10 years of medical practice and an unparalleled spirit of entrepreneurship to master the art of following speeches closely and then printing out cohesive and meaningful transcripts. With time, she established processes to make the work simpler and became one of the most efficient transcriptionists. When her husband moved to a suburb, Linh Chun joined him. Moving into the suburbs was a welcome change. However, the suburban peace came at a cost—the cost of disconnecting from her transcription clients. As she had not established a strong sales channel, she had to join the local elementary school. The elementary school was run by an entrepreneur who had limited knowledge of practices at other schools. Two days after Linh joined the school, she had asked for a procedure manual. Baffled, the entrepreneur had asked back, "What manual?"

Rajiv Sinha moved back to India after getting an MBA from an American University. With his parents' insistence that he stay close to the family, he gave up a six-figure salary in the States to take an offer in New Delhi. Rajiv was helping a friend of his father's grow a textile manufacturing company. With the advent of American, German, Japanese, and Korean global giants in India, the commute was smooth and efficiency of life had changed significantly.

The Indian entrepreneur knew all his suppliers and clients; however, he failed to document all this information. He had always been successful using his (archaic) ways, and so he questioned the extra hassle of writing things down. The price lists also resided in the entrepreneur's head. Nobody in the firm had any idea of how changing one parameter within the firm might impact the other ones. The onus of connecting the dots now fell on Rajiv. Rajiv had to make the entrepreneur understand the importance of being growth-ready and establish stronger controls. It took over two years for Rajiv to gather and aggregate the information to develop and implement meaningful controls within the firm.

We can see from these examples how important it is to have well-defined processes and a knowledge base so that these could be disseminated within the firm. This Procedural section highlights how to implement controls within firms, with existing resources and under current conditions. After all, undistinguished entrepreneurial firms do not often have processes and methodologies in place, and even if they do, the undistinguished entrepreneur overrules them every now and then.

Undistinguished entrepreneurs could diverge from the goals of the firm almost every day, thereby stunting the firm's growth. Imagine the undistinguished entrepreneur asking you to sell a completely new product that your company has never dealt with and that the entrepreneur heard about on the radio while driving to work. Does this situation seem familiar?

A research study conducted by a team under Neil Churchill (currently Professor Emeritus of Entrepreneurship at INSEAD, France) at Southern Methodist University, found that small businesses experience similar problems at different stages of development.[4] The team developed a framework for five stages of development, described by management factors such as managerial style, organizational structure, formal systems, goals, and owner's involvement:

1. **Existence Stage:** This is the first stage where the owner's focus is to obtain customers and deliver them the product.
2. **Survival Stage:** This is where the owner's key problem shifts to keeping a balance between revenues and expenses.
3. **Success Stage:** At this stage, the company grows and the key question for the owner is to either grow it further or disengage from it.
4. **Take-off Stage:** If the company has reached the take-off stage, its key question is how to grow rapidly and fund that growth.
5. **Resource Maturity Stage:** At this stage, the company should consolidate the gains and sustain its advantages, including its entrepreneurial spirit.

The undistinguished entrepreneur perpetually struggles in stages 1 and 2, and rarely reaches stage 3. Perhaps the lack of formal systems and procedures could be one contributing factor for not making it there. This is where you come in to get the firm to stages 3 and 4.

It seems that among the majority of standard procedures that ended up on the undistinguished entrepreneurs' doorsteps, only a few made it to the company manuals. Many entrepreneurial firms give employee reviews, issue paychecks (generally on time), and allow some vacations here and there (perhaps to convince doubtful employees, which result in confusing them even further); but overall, they lack the most important ingredient for success, which I call the

SF, or the *Sustenance Factor*. Despite its near-invisibility (and intangibility), the SF is an extremely important ingredient in such growing firms, and the lack of it makes what could be a great place to work, a mediocre one.

The SF of any firm can be improved by following the procedural rules in this section.

■

1

Early to work has its perk(s)

HAVE we become so transfixed by flexible schedules that we have completely given up on traditional discipline? Perhaps you might have too—the undistinguished entrepreneur, however, has not.

Most undistinguished entrepreneurs are pacesetters with a coercive style of leadership. They like compliance and sticking to (their) high standards. And so, arriving on time becomes a part of employee discipline but leaving on time is considered the employee's responsibility.

There has never been a substitute for hard work, professionalism, and devotion to a firm, but there is nothing wrong in managing one's work intelligently. In order to set a procedure, work within the schedule—arrive and leave on time and keep the entrepreneur informed that you are working hard to attain project goals (goals that might not have been realistic and realizable at the outset).

Staying late may signal to the entrepreneur that you are ready to take on more responsibility, but, conversely, staying late can also reflect negatively on your sharpness and efficiency, particularly if you are given the same amount of responsibility as your coworkers. If you do stay late, give the entrepreneur a heads up about the specifics; that will go a long way in proving that you are working hard to offset unwise promises (not yours) that were made when the project was defined.

It is not a bad idea to take one-hour lunches for recuperating and reenergizing. Also, never carry work outside the office unless you are paid or specifically requested to do so—that will help preserve your "smart employee" image.

Although I cannot recommend a quick and easy solution to such discipline checks, particularly if the entrepreneur is of the spying type, I have met several employees who experimented with various methods to make it look as if they were still at work during the late hours. Among the notable ones are:

- Leaving the computer on with an Excel sheet displayed to show some of the projects they have been working on

- Leaving keys on the desk (it's important to have an extra set of car keys)
- Leaving a briefcase in an obvious place (one employee alternated between taking it home and keeping it in the office)

A research team led by Daniel Goleman, a leading author and science journalist, found that coercive, pacesetting leaders (including many undistinguished entrepreneurs) negatively impact the work climate and cause lower financial returns.[5] So, before the undistinguished entrepreneur causes any negative impact around you, tighten your work schedule at the very minimum.

2

Set job descriptions and employer expectations

THERE *is never enough time to do it right the first time, but there is always enough time to do it again*. This adage seems to apply to the work philosophy of the undistinguished entrepreneur. For the undistinguished entrepreneur, it is much easier to correct errors after they occur than to take the time upfront to define what is needed.

As soon as Rajiv learned that all the Rolodex contacts for the company were sitting inside the undistinguished entrepreneur's head, he made the undistinguished entrepreneur abreast of how he was envisioning the flow of information to be and also ways to communicate with prospect customers. The entrepreneur had never taken the initiative to inform Rajiv about his client management procedures and was skeptical of the new ways Rajiv proposed.

One key reason for such misalignment of expectations between the employee and the undistinguished entrepreneur is that the entrepreneur never takes the time to relate what he or she wants, but nonetheless assumes that the employee will produce a 100 percent quality delivery. The undistinguished entrepreneur has forgotten to describe what this 100 percent should entail and at the project end, fault-finding becomes imminent.

Employees are not mind readers. They should be informed of what their responsibilities are and what the entrepreneur expects of them. Through my interviews, I have seen that most employees at entrepreneurial firms do not set expectations very well; too often, they are hired and the very next day put on a project, without much orientation.

However, if the undistinguished entrepreneur does not specify expectations or roles, you as an employee have to be proactive in defining them.

- Discuss priorities, roles, and action plans to provide a common understanding for setting goals and expectations.
- Conduct periodic update meetings to keep the undistinguished entrepreneur on track. During these meetings, you can share project status and suggest changes in priorities.
- Initiate one-on-one meetings to review work in progress. At these meetings, review potential issues before they snowball into large ones.

In a changing economy, employees are more attuned to survival and loyalty than to challenging the undistinguished entrepreneur who is using wrong methods. Asking the undistinguished entrepreneur to sign a contract might seem risky, but it will not be the end of his or her world. An employee contract retains talent and encourages performance. The contract should clearly define responsibilities; state the hours, vacation time, and holidays; and even include a termination agreement. Other potential conflicts need to be covered in the contract as well to leave room for mutually acceptable resolutions.

Can you change the calendar now...We are in June...be a little organized
MAY 08
K
Shil

3

Preach against micromanagement and encourage delegation

ARE you watched constantly and often asked for the intricate details of your tasks? Are you afraid that if you do not update him or her constantly and ask for direction, the undistinguished entrepreneur will get upset? In either case, you are being micromanaged and you need to curb that practice.

The undistinguished entrepreneur operates from a belief that employees are incapable of following through on the tasks assigned to them. This is a morale killer for employees. Micromanagement restricts the ability to evolve and grow, and it also limits what a team can achieve because everything has to go through one person.

You know the undistinguished entrepreneur is micromanaging when, he is:

- Not delegating at all
- Discouraging actions without his or her consent
- Perpetually overseeing everyone at work
- Delving into minute details and ignoring the big picture

- Taking back delegated work before it is finished if he or she senses the slightest problem
- Triangulating with other employees and collecting internal intelligence

Most of the time, the undistinguished entrepreneur does not even realize he or she is micromanaging. He gets focused on his own little agenda, which sends employees chasing around after details instead of getting work done. The undistinguished entrepreneur does not allow employees to set or keep the priorities for accomplishing their daily goals, and on top of that, he or she questions their time-management abilities.

Starting as a do-all entrepreneur (in the existence and survival stages we discussed earlier), the undistinguished entrepreneur continues in the do-all mode. As the organization grows, however, this habit becomes very unsustainable. The entrepreneur needs to be transitioned to the next level, in which he or she delegates more work to the leaders in the organization while focusing on longer-range planning himself (or herself).

Here are a few things that you can do to help the entrepreneur through these transitions:

- Help the entrepreneur to set milestones and use them to check progress.
- Build trust by giving the entrepreneur examples of how you saved the boat from sinking in the past.
- Get assigned to projects that you are confident about—this will catapult you into the entrepreneur's circle of trust.
- Delegate work by encouraging the entrepreneur to assess others' strengths and skills.
- Provide status reports regularly to discourage his spying and triangulating.

Neither Rome nor a successful business was built in a day. The undistinguished entrepreneur cannot change overnight, so gain his trust and be patient.

4

Provide information proactively

DAVID HANSEN worked with mainframes for more than 20 years before he decided to start his own information technology (IT) firm in Southern California, specializing in programming in a Microsoft environment. He had always told friends that he wanted to settle in sunny Orange County, and the move was not that difficult. Hiring movers was inexpensive in a down economy.

The shift from mainframes to server-based solutions, however, was a much more radical change. David was confronted with, not only a new technology, but also a more aggressive approach to programming. He now had competition from a multitude of platforms and service providers. His quest for a breakthrough software-as-a-service (SaaS) product in a cutthroat market kept him overly occupied, with one thought after the other. Focused on attaining success, he did not attend to his existing projects nor did he support his key operations. As a result, a few existing clients did not get what they wanted and subsequently complained—loudly and clearly.

When David got a negative feedback from his clients, he went on a rampage and tore into his employees. After calming down, he revisited every corner to seek information on what all fell through the cracks. He took every possible measure to control damage and instituted an open-door policy for his employees. Gradually, things changed for the better.

This scenario has been reenacted at other entrepreneurial firms as well, and has taught us some lessons; the most important one being: *A frustrated entrepreneur, if informed of problems only at the eleventh hour, cannot handle them.* It is good to be proactive in all your work—and even better to keep the undistinguished entrepreneur informed about projects, including those in which you might face difficulties.

The undistinguished entrepreneur, on an average, listens to only the first 15 or 20 words of what you have to say, due to preoccupation with his or her own thoughts. It isn't possible to have 10 things on your mind at once, but the undistinguished entrepreneur seems to do just that, and at the same time, be absorbed in plans for establishing peace and prosperity in the world. So, to be on the safe side, check yourself and start using shorter sentences. Also, insert attention-getters such as "doable" or "profitable" in those 15 words. And as the undistinguished entrepreneur has the tendency to ask "Why?" after almost everything you say, be prepared with reasons.

If you need to ask for personal consideration at times, it is a good idea to inform the undistinguished entrepreneur ahead of time and try to establish a rapport that only the two of you share. You may need to report your toothache and an upcoming dental visit, or the fact that your dearest niece is about to be married in Argentina before you actually ask for time off. However, do not divulge too much information or it will seem that you are becoming overly familiar (either because you want a promotion or you are trying to put a cover on some major disaster that you just committed).

Being proactive in communicating with the undistinguished entrepreneur not only saves you from the aftermath of potential failure, but also provides him or her with complete visibility of the real circumstances of a situation. It builds trust and

establishes a solid partnership between the entrepreneur and you. A positive outcome of this partnership can come in the form of understanding the entrepreneur's needs and managing the day-to-day firefighting with him. That aside, it also helps teach the undistinguished entrepreneur to micromanage less.

5

Practice the golden scrub savers

SAM COOPER was a self-proclaimed turnaround expert. When he was hired by the undistinguished entrepreneur of a small consulting business in engineering services, Sam brought rules for all employees with him to the very first meeting. Sam distributed the rules without knowing much about the firm, the entrepreneur, or the employees. What he did was similar to what some medical practitioners do when they prescribe antibiotics without diagnosing the ailment—he used the same tools he had used at other companies, without assessing the problems he was hired to fix. Initially, he was taken seriously and considered to be the entrepreneur's right hand; but within two months, he was let go by the same entrepreneur.

Employees felt stressed while working with Sam because they felt that his goals were unrealizable and his assumptions were all over the place. He would yell at employees if they did not do what he asked, and he showed no understanding of the workflow or the business.

Sam, however, did a few things right. He taught the employees the use of TACTIC scrub savers—that would help you every time, no matter who you deal with at the firm (particularly the undistinguished entrepreneur):

- Never over-**T**alk. If you talk too much, the undistinguished entrepreneur will feel that the extra talk is there to compensate for poor work.
- Never get **A**ngry. Never let your frustration drive you to act against the undistinguished entrepreneur. Remember who signs your paychecks.
- Never **C**ry. Crying could signal that you are weak and can be controlled.
- Never give **T**oo Much Information (TMI). Doing so just opens you up to further questioning, which is a can of worms you did not prepare for.
- Never be too **I**nformal. It is good to be friendly and tell a few jokes every now and then, but talking about your friend's bachelor party or how you survived on beer for a week in college does not appropriately reflect your professionalism or your commitment to grow the firm.
- Never get too **C**lose. Showing too much care about the undistinguished entrepreneur's personal life might detract from your merit. However, this does not apply if the undistinguished entrepreneur is sick or has a car with a problem. In fact, those might be the best times to show some kindness.

Sam could have made great friends at work (and been retained longer) if he had worked on his methods of giving feedback and tried to develop some emotional intelligence, rather than handing out a laundry list of prescription medicines for a yet-to-be-diagnosed pain. But his TACTIC scrub savers outlived him among the employees.

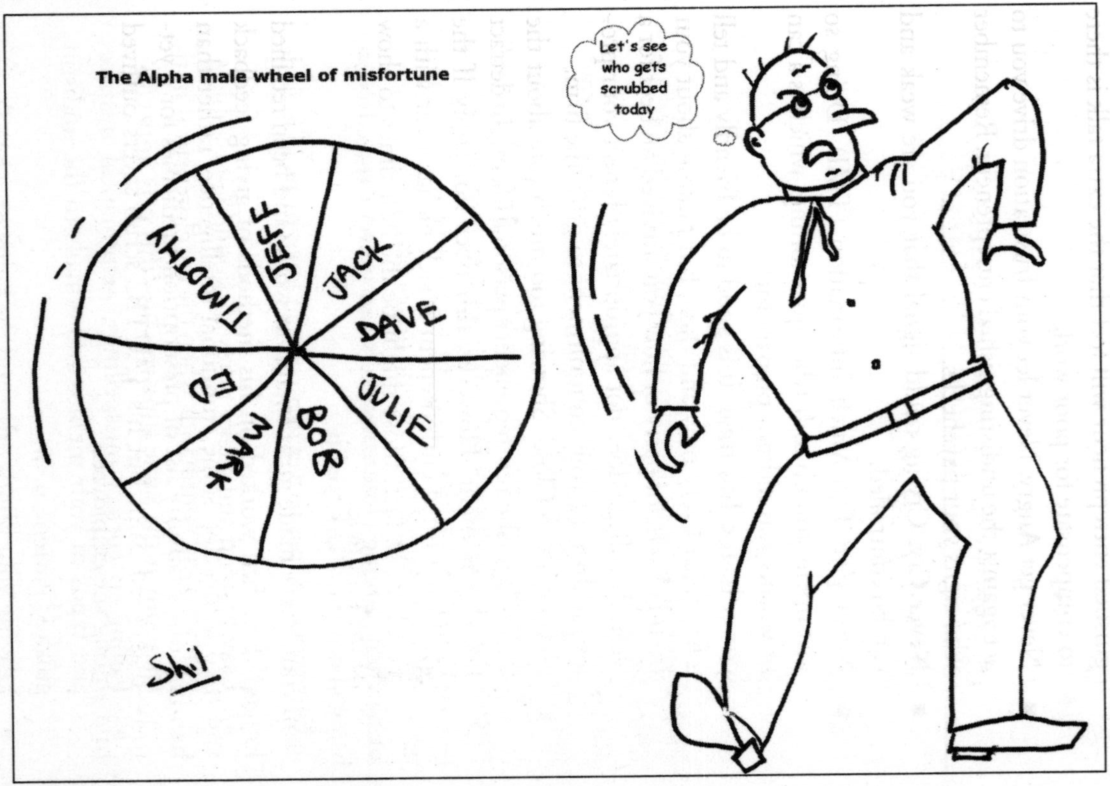
The Alpha male wheel of misfortune
TIMOTHY
JEFF
JACK
DAVE
JULIE
BOB
MARK
ED
Let's see who gets scrubbed today
Shil

6

Avoid becoming the target of pet peeves

HAVE you been called in to the undistinguished entrepreneur's office for a one-on-one disciplining session just because you left the lights on when you left work the previous evening? If not, consider yourself lucky.

There are many less fortunate people who work with undistinguished entrepreneurs but fail to realize how small things can come back and bite them. In such situations, making a list of the undistinguished entrepreneur's pet peeves and circulating them among close coworkers can prevent tragedies and bring about more collegiality.

Entrepreneurs' pet peeves that you can learn to avoid include:

- Leaving food and sticky notes all around your cubicle.
- Not washing your hands when the entrepreneur is in the restroom at the same time you are (this gets noticed!).
- Failing to correct misspellings, grammatical mistakes, and typos in your memos and e-mails to the undistinguished entrepreneur.
- Leaving your blinds open and the lights on when leaving work.
- Abusing sick leave and getting caught doing so.

- Covering your cubicle with your accomplishments and your favorites.
- Setting your computer to emit noises every time you click your mouse or log in.
- Receiving frequent personal phone calls at work.

By taking the entrepreneur's pet peeves into account, you are staying within the norms defined by the entrepreneur. These may not be written as rules in the contract or the employee manual, but they have the same propensity to take you down if you do not live by them.

7

Prevent fires: Keep your schedule visible

SAM was let go, and his successor, Juan Lopez, worked to increase visibility and transparency within the firm. He initiated whiteboard writing, created a project management status website, and implemented knowledge-sharing applications within the firm.

Juan knew that scheduling is an important procedure, not only for keeping the undistinguished entrepreneur updated, but also for enabling team members to organize themselves before potential conflicts or prioritizing lapses occur. Lapses can result in project disasters and bad client relations, and ultimately send a firm's reputation into freefall. The majority of small firms or brands that end up nowhere got started in that direction with small lapses.

The undistinguished entrepreneurial firms often take what seems to be an unusually long time to deliver a product. During that time, the customer may lose patience (and respect) or the firm may feel pressured to deliver a product that has not been tested thoroughly. For the most part, project managers ignore the customer complaints and try to provide what the undistinguished entrepreneur typically wants—more revenue for less work performed. Some project managers, however, muster the courage to keep a visible schedule and serve the customer better. It is during these times that the employees make the entrepreneur realize the importance of transparent scheduling and regaining confidence of the customers.

Once Juan had assured himself that everyone was working according to his or her assigned role, he started a "results or reasons" campaign to make employees more answerable for their work and to uncover scope creep on assigned projects. That brought to the surface another question: were employees carrying out their roles correctly?

Doing work not within one's assigned areas of responsibility has two faces. It can either be a positive extension of a role or indicate a dysfunction within the organization. To ensure that the outcome is positive, meet with the entrepreneur and gain familiarity with what is in scope—and what is not—before you begin. Failure to understand the scope of a job can lead you to do things that you are not expected to and wreak havoc with your timeline.

T.J. Rodgers, founder and CEO of Cypress Semiconductor, grew a successful company by using a simple goal-based system, without any complex computer algorithms.[6] The employees at Cypress set their own goals and priorities every week. By comparing goals and disparities, the management was able to visualize problems, identify problem trends, and put the company back on course before crises could arise.

Schedules can be designed around projects, both short term and long term. With limited resources, priorities must be guarded carefully, and the entrepreneur must understand the need to keep variances (and their impact) at a minimum.

The Project Management Institute (www.pmi.org) offers resources on managing schedules and team resources.[7] Use these as well as other project management resources to keep tabs on scope, schedule, budget, quality, and transparency so that the undistinguished entrepreneur can see where failures might occur.

8

Discourage bonding through sports or social networks

IT is very important to periodically assess *all* relationships—who you depend on and who all depend on you. In addition to such assessments, you should also work to bridge differences. And what is better than a game of racquetball to do that?

For ages, sports and games have been a vital component of society. Historically, playing was not just about having fun; it also had practical benefits: it formed bonds that solidified the group. In addition, it had stress-reducing and other health benefits.

In modern days, racquetball and similar team or paired sports may increase metabolism, but when it comes to bonding with the undistinguished entrepreneur, do not consider sports as a means for doing so. Think of joining a gym and going there regularly for cardio exercise or weights instead. Playing a game or sport with the undistinguished entrepreneur every other day removes professionalism from the relationship.

If the entrepreneur makes a request, you can certainly play a few games. The same goes for every other sport, including golf. If the entrepreneur keeps on asking though, you should cite prior engagements and beg off in a way that causes no hard feelings.

With social networks booming, you might even receive a "friend" request from the entrepreneur. In that case you can accept, but examine your convictions (and your reason) before putting all your tacky pictures on those sites. It is very difficult to ignore any request, and especially a friend request, from the person who pays your wages. But be careful before airing your dirty laundry in public.

While your work and personal relationships will inevitably intersect at certain junctures, remember that there is a difference between the people you call buddies (or friends) and the undistinguished entrepreneur.

9

Don't buy expensive gifts—they *will* really *cost you!*

JIM ROSE was an accountant at his parents' mom-and-pop bookstore. With the advent of publishing and distribution conglomerates, the smaller bookstores started disappearing (a theme depicted in the popular 1998 Hollywood movie *You've Got Mail*). When Jim's family business ran into debts and eventually went bankrupt, Jim moved over to an entrepreneurial firm, as an accountant—a QuickBooks expert.

Jim had the habit of spending outrageously on gifts for the shop owner and sometimes even for his coworkers. The entrepreneur was fine with Jim's work but felt uncomfortable about Jim's extravagant and unnecessary gifts. One day when the entrepreneur discovered a small problem in the accounting books, he snapped at Jim. Three months later, after a similar incident, he let Jim go. Jim's habit had created mistrust and suspicion of his accounting skills in the entrepreneur's mind.

It is a good idea to give gifts to the undistinguished entrepreneur only at times when they might reasonably be called for, for example, an important anniversary or birthday.

According to Noah Goldstein of UCLA's Anderson School of Management, the author of *Yes!: 50 Scientifically Proven Ways to Be Persuasive* (2008), gifts should be given unconditionally and without any expectation of reciprocity.[8] Furthermore, gifts should be significant, customized, and unexpected. So every time you send a Christmas chocolate bag to the entrepreneur, think again if that is really a surprise.

For strengthening a bond with the undistinguished entrepreneur, cordiality and thankfulness are the keys. A dinner would be a perfect setting and a great gesture. Ask the entrepreneur's spouse to join the two of you for a dinner at one of his or her favorite restaurants. Start with wine and never show signs of frugality, even if every request from the menu gives you a small panic attack about the final check.

If you are representing a group of employees who are buying a collective gift for the undistinguished entrepreneur, brainstorm with the group and give him or her something that

will last for a long time and serve as a reminder of the group (including you). Group photos, sports accessories, office appliances, or even software can go a long way toward pleasing the entrepreneur.

Be it sports, gifts or any other way, bonding with the undistinguished entrepreneur is the best investment you can make. The results are better and surer than even those of investing in high-return AAA-rated securities.

10

Let what happens at home stay at home

IN addition to his habit of trying to buy favor with gifts, Jim Rose also had a habit of talking about the details of his personal life with his coworkers and with the undistinguished entrepreneur. Making every detail public did Jim no good in terms of promoting his accounting knowledge or demonstrating how hard he worked. On the contrary, it reflected that Jim's personal life was distracting him from his work.

It is true that maintaining a great relationship with the undistinguished entrepreneur demands you be a conversation starter at times. It is not bad to give information about your brother's new job and how the industry in which he works is doing. However, it is too much to keep your boss updated with the details of your last social network meeting and the politics of that group, and how you impressed everyone there with your fluency in Spanish. And talking about the people you dated over the past year is a definite no.

While the undistinguished entrepreneur might be sympathetic about your spouse leaving you, perpetual complaints about personal issues will make you seem unstable, unreliable, and a crybaby. Put on your big-boy pants! Yes, that is what you should do when you feel an uncontrollable urge to talk on and on. But what happens if the entrepreneur is chattier than you?

If that is the case, you have to be watchful of your words. You run the risk of your personal information becoming a featured item in the undistinguished entrepreneur's babble to someone else. If the undistinguished entrepreneur is chatting away with you, you must make it clear in the most civil way that you do not want to participate.

There are socially acceptable methods for getting the undistinguished entrepreneur to break the TMI habit.

- If you are in an office (as opposed to a cubicle), keep the door closed or nearly closed. An open door is an invitation to an unending conversation.
- If you are already in a conversation that has lost its path, you can politely put forth the fact that you are afraid of falling behind on tasks and do not want to let the entrepreneur down.
- You can also begin an exit routine. Stand up, and then continue listening but move slowly out of your office as if you have to get a document from the printer or meet with a coworker on another project.

MY RELATIONSHIPS

11

No bypassing

DAVID HANSEN, the IT entrepreneur in Orange County, California, saw an immediate change in the organization after he instituted an open-door policy. Clients were happier because David was more involved. The firm's focus changed toward better service, and David started assigning roles and responsibilities in a much better way.

David wanted to ensure that all decisions flowed without delay through the organization. He went to the extent of assigning signature authorities to free up his time for management responsibilities. However, he still wanted to be kept informed about every significant event or transaction.

Undistinguished entrepreneurs such as David never accept being out of the loop—even if they want *you* to make the decision. You find yourself having to inform the undistinguished entrepreneur about almost every transaction—a US$ 5 purchase of packing tape as well as closure of a million-dollar deal.

At Cypress Semiconductor, the management solved this problem by allocating a weekly budget to every manager.[9] Every week, at a purchase order meeting, they looked for questionable expenditures. With such a tracking mechanism, there was no need to get the CEO's permission to act on decisions most of the time; just every once in a while.

With the same idea, a good first step would be to discuss with the undistinguished entrepreneur if you can get some decision-making authority for contingencies. In the discussion, bring up the fact that the undistinguished entrepreneur assigned you your responsibilities so that he or she could be freed up for other management activities.

Another way to ensure that the entrepreneur does not feel bypassed by your decision is by redirecting the success to him or her when your efforts are successful. You can thank the undistinguished entrepreneur and acknowledge that the triumph was entirely due to his or her giving you the opportunity and exposure.

However, you can be a subject of bypassing as well. Your subordinates may be bypassing *you* and reporting to the undistinguished entrepreneur. The entrepreneur may even be asking them to do so, knowingly or unknowingly. The best way to stop this trend is to ask the entrepreneur not to discuss with your subordinates any issue that you can handle and to redirect such issues through you. Subordinates will ultimately realize that bypassing you is not working, and they will stop.

If you cannot get the undistinguished entrepreneur to back you up, there is a good chance that he or she has either insufficient knowledge of your tasks or limited trust in your capabilities. In that case, you have to speak with him or her, clarify your responsibilities, and demonstrate that you have ample technical know-how and people-management skills to lead the tasks.

12

Use positive feedback to build a team

AS the undistinguished entrepreneur so often has a trust issue (never trusting anyone), he or she practices triangulation to build better control into the environment. The undistinguished entrepreneur might ask you about your coworkers and then ask them about you. I call this triangulation because the entrepreneur tries to confirm a fact by referring to two or more persons.

Triangulation is a necessary step for surveying a piece of land. However, if instead of land-surveying equipment the triangulation relies on what employees report, those employees better be aware how critical their reporting can be to a coworker's career. The key is to keep a good working relationship with everyone. And giving good feedback about others helps even more. Expectations, trust, and influence take time to get established. But don't wait to start building relationships at work, start right away.

When Rajiv Sinha found that the entrepreneur he worked with in India was not going to provide him with necessary information about processes and policies, he did not pick the entrepreneur's brain any further. Instead, he made friends in the firm. Employees at first rejected Rajiv's improvement ideas. They didn't believe that someone fresh out of school could "teach us how to do our jobs."

To combat that attitude, Rajiv set up one-on-one lunches with each employee. He shared with them how he had learned to make dyes during his engineering college days and the mistakes he made there, among other such stories. With great humility, he asked employees about their plans in regard to the firm, how they saw the firm developing over the next five years, and how they thought the firm should move ahead. Rajiv received many ideas from the employees to make the processes better. Rajiv took those ideas to the entrepreneur and walked him through possible implementations. Soon, Rajiv had made everyone a partner in the growth process and was well on his way to building a solid team.

One useful approach to developing good teams is the Forming–Storming–Norming–Performing approach proposed by Bruce Tuckman in 1965. He maintained that these phases were necessary for the team to form (bring their individual talents), storm (face each other and resolve differences), norm (plan common goals and find joint solutions), and perform (execute effectively and deliver results).

Team-building can generate shared values and eventually support the strategies needed to achieve goals. Effective team-building inculcates discipline and brings about better coordination and a collective maturity among the team members.

From my interactions with small businesses, I have noticed that team-building does not happen as naturally in smaller entrepreneurial firms as it does in bigger corporations. Often, the culture in smaller firms does not recognize or support a lot of collaboration. However, in firms where both the "group IQ" and individual emotional IQs are well developed, there is more harmony and a stronger network, both critical in facing unanticipated problems.

As team development is not always considered a high priority at every entrepreneurial firm, you can initiate one at yours by using some GUESSWORK!

Goal-and-role review with team members
Update skills of team members
Empower team members with broader scope
Set expectations
Sympathize and empathize with the team
Work together—interact and relate
Openly communicate
Remember wins and celebrate accomplishments
Knowledge share

13

Be assertive in your communication

COMMUNICATION is very important at the undistinguished enterprise and the fact that you are good at it is a likely reason that you were selected for your job. Even then, it is important to build the undistinguished entrepreneur's confidence in you before he or she goes into an introspective state and starts questioning the quality of your work.

Linh Chun, the Chinese elementary schoolteacher, did not get the manual she needed so badly when she requested it from the entrepreneur. The other teachers in the school were not inclined to help her with an orientation either. The previous owner of the school had not left a succession plan nor shown any interest in the school's continuing operation. The entrepreneur who took over the school was a philanthropist and he did not want students to lose out on the elementary education. However, as running a school was different from the entrepreneur's experience in managing business organizations, he did not have the knowledge to manage his new enterprise.

Linh Chun had transcription experience, but she was new to schools herself. Without asking for too much, she tried to help the situation and stepped up the establishment of procedures. She identified that more communication would bring more interaction within the school faculty and with the customers, thus bringing out the needs, issues, and pain points of the organization. As the renewed emphasis on communication was okayed by the entrepreneur, Linh set up communication channels between the entrepreneur, coworkers, and parents of the students and laid out communication policies to identify needs and help resolve issues quickly.

As meetings started getting time consuming and expensive —particularly when multiple people spent multiple hours in multiple meetings—she put emphasis on e-mailing and resolving issues as they occur, thus reducing the need for meetings. With all that information she gathered through e-mails and meetings, she not only crafted a framework for handling issues and designed policies/procedures for school operation but also put out protocols and policies on communication.

Here are a few communication protocols you might want to follow to more effectively resolve issues in your organization:

- **E-mail the undistinguished entrepreneur before you meet in person**
  If you become aware of an issue, e-mail the information to the entrepreneur and subsequently inform in person. If the entrepreneur e-mails you, react immediately. Use carbon copying (cc) carefully to avoid humiliating him or her by mistake. Double-check your e-mails to see if there is anything in what you've written that ridicules the undistinguished entrepreneur or presents your ideas inappropriately.
- **Prepare before a meeting**
  When meeting the undistinguished entrepreneur to ask for something or to present an update, prepare by asking yourself the following questions:
  - What is that you want to ask?
  - Why do you want to ask that?
  - Is the timing right? Would another time be better?
  - Could your ideas create or bring out a conflict?
  - Do you have any helpful supplemental information?
  - Is there a possible resolution already available that you want to make the entrepreneur aware of?
  - Can you explain the situation in more detail if the entrepreneur asks you to elaborate?
- **Assert yourself in the meeting**
  In a meeting, as in all communication, be assertive. Do not just sit back and enjoy the meetings. Research the issues, review or prepare an agenda, and come to the meeting with a list of questions that relate to the topics to be discussed. Show your enthusiasm but be succinct. Your communication should show persistence, insight, and patience, as opposed to frustration.

Here are a couple of other things to keep in mind for meetings:

- State the negatives or drawbacks first and then the positives that offset the negatives.[10] A statement such as: "We did better than others even though we accomplished only 50 percent of our goals" is better stated as: "Our performance was not as strong as we had expected, but despite all the supplier problems, we still achieved 50 percent of our goals, which was better than others in the industry."
- Demonstrate to the entrepreneur that you have made progress so that he or she sees the need to follow through.[11] In endowed progress effect experiments, conducted by Joseph C. Nunes of the University of Southern California and Xavier Drèze of the Wharton School, observed how some car-wash companies retain customers: when they offer a punch card that gives a regular customer a free wash after, say, eight washes, they will occasionally make an extra click after a wash. This makes the customer see progress more quickly and encourages him or her to continue toward the goal of getting a free wash.

By being positive and showing that you are on your path of achievement, you help the entrepreneur visualize where he can help and ideate to make your path even easier.

14

Understand that personal favors can hurt you

JIM ROSE, from our earlier bookstore example, had yet another habit. He frequently asked for small favors from the entrepreneur and other coworkers, particularly favors of a personal nature. Jim used to call in sick almost every month (he was actually playing football with his friends), even during the peak book-buying season. Jim also took up a side job for commissions with a pyramid product-sales company and even asked the entrepreneur to buy these products.

If you really do need a favor, don't ask the entrepreneur; ask people you have helped or your friends. Think of your right to favors as a credit pool in which you have a limit of three favors. If you ask the entrepreneur for three small favors—a ride home, jump-starting your car, and taking you to a lunch—you exhaust all your favor-credit points. Just imagine how difficult it will be now to ask for more meaningful things, such as a raise, extra vacation days, or a flexible work schedule.

Be aware also that if you introduce your friends and family to the entrepreneur and they later ask the entrepreneur for small favors, those favors also count against your (three) credits.

None of this is to say that the entrepreneur will not ask favors of *you*. Entrepreneurs can ask you to pick them up for lunch or take their children to school before you come to work. So long as this occurs only once in a while, it is okay; but do not let the requests become repetitive. Approach the undistinguished entrepreneur as though you were a peer rather than as a subordinate and politely refuse requests with a convincing excuse (your spouse is waiting for you, your dog is suffering from a fever, or another similar reason). And then thank the undistinguished entrepreneur for valuing your services.

If you do end up granting a favor, make sure that it is perceived as significant and not forgotten. According to Noah Goldstein at UCLA's Anderson School of Management, favor-granting has a defect he calls asymmetric perception[12]—wine to the favor-doer can be perceived as bread by the favor-receiver—you may think you provided very critical information to the undistinguished entrepreneur while the entrepreneur feels he or she received something that was not of much value.

Another problem is memory decay;[13] over time, the entrepreneur forgets your favor. So if you do a favor, make sure that you give gentle reminders of it afterward, as needed. Managing favors in this way can bring about a positive change in the relationship between you and the undistinguished entrepreneur.

Thanks for the jump start - I should be okay now!
Shil

15

Use office resources only for office purposes

SAM COOPER, the self-proclaimed turnaround expert of our earlier example, had a long list of friends that he called every morning from his office at the engineering consulting firm. He would tell them how badly other companies had been bleeding before he arrived to turn them around and made them into money-minting machines. He was completely oblivious to the fact that his self-advertisement did not sit well with the entrepreneur. In addition to this, Sam was using office time and office resources to glorify himself.

Undistinguished entrepreneurs are very conscious of what they consider unauthorized use of their limited resources. If you need to photocopy a personal document, print out an itinerary for your trip to Hawaii, or borrow a car for an evening on the town with an old friend, think twice before using company resources.

Making personal calls from the office phone during work hours counts as a double misuse—you are using your billable hours and you are abusing your rights to the company phone plan. It is a good idea to avoid use of company resources completely, even after office hours. Remember, these unauthorized uses stack up in a negative way, just as personal favors do. Also, they bring about the perception that you are taking productive time and resources from the company and investing them in yourself.

Few would argue against the need for a good work–life balance, but in the work environment, too much attention to your personal life is just as likely to destroy the balance as too much work at home. If you are busy sending instant messages to your daughter or your spouse when the entrepreneur stops by your office or cubicle, you are inviting trouble. Even worse, if you frequently visit a social networking site and have a huge list of your fans to keep up with.

We all goof off from time to time and being away from work while *at* work can sometimes increase productivity. However, getting caught is embarrassing. To avoid that, avoid these while at work:

- Checking your personal e-mail or forwarding jokes to friends
- Reading the news online
- Checking the status of your investments and other accounts or paying bills online

- Playing games online or catching up on TV programs you missed
- Performing web searches on people you used to know
- Holding on to project files to make it look like you are working while making personal calls or sending personal e-mail
- Searching for a better job

If you have been frittering away your hours for a while and want to know whether the entrepreneur has noticed, try the Quick Preoccupied Walk (QPW). Walk past the undistinguished entrepreneur's office without conversation or even eye contact, looking serious to indicate that you are working on something important. The QPW acts as a confirmation to the undistinguished entrepreneur that you are on an important task.

16

Treat important tasks as projects to manage

NO matter how experienced or skillful you are at managing tasks to perfection, unforeseen events will often rear their menacing head and create roadblocks. Treating all tasks as projects to be managed can sometimes help. You can do this by defining scope, schedule, cost, quality, and resource requirements, whenever feasible. This approach will help you recognize potential issues, enact contingency plans, mobilize resources, and reward the team for its successes.

Sam Cooper's successor, Juan Lopez, created a project status website, which brought about greater accountability. Juan's Six Sigma Black Belt experience also helped him leverage that learning to streamline issue management by:

- Defining the project by listening to the client and identifying the aspects that are critical to quality.
- Measuring key steps in the workflows and processes, collecting relevant data, and identifying frequency of issues/defects.
- Analyzing the data to investigate and identify the root cause of the problems and trends in defects—why, when, and where do the issues/defects occur.

- Improving and optimizing the current process with a creative improvement plan. Juan made sure that the improvement plan ideas came from the employees.
- Controlling and sustaining the processes (under the improved plan) to ensure that any variances are corrected before they result in issues.

Project management traces its origins to the fields of construction, engineering, and defense, where planning, resource use, and time management are key drivers. The International Project Management Association (IPMA) in Europe, the Project Management Institute (PMI) in the United States, and other similar organizations around the world stress the importance of initiating, planning, executing, monitoring, and reaching closure in project management.

T.J. Rodgers has explained how the goal system at Cypress Semiconductor replaced bureaucratic obscurity with visibility and helped solve problems.[14] The goal system included developing a task description and determining the priorities, owner, and supervisor for all projects—the basis of any project management system.

If you look back at the earlier chapters, we learned that both Rajiv Sinha and Linh Chun had also taken the initiative to redefine the projects and prioritize tasks, even under resource constraints, to help the firms focus on the Critical Customer Requirements. They also made considerable effort in improving and optimizing existing processes by strengthening communication and cohesiveness within their teams.

Right from the start, Rajiv and Linh looked at all these tasks as projects and followed through on them, from initiation to closure. Even after closure, they continued to champion their causes and sustained the improvements.

17

Share knowledge and train coworkers

ON-THE-JOB learning starts with looking into what other leading firms—local and global—are doing and what new technologies are available in the market.

Rajiv Sinha began his on-the-job learning by exploring the best engineering practices in textile mills. He also toyed with the idea of outsourcing work to other companies that could perform them in a more cost-effective way. He examined leasing agreements to look for alternate ways to manage property, plant, and equipment expenses for expansion plans. Rajiv spoke with industry leaders and textile gurus, visited trade shows, and shared his thoughts with both the entrepreneur and his coworkers. This self-education and due diligence helped him to think outside the undistinguished box.

Getting oneself educated and then transferring the knowledge to others is perceived as an even more important aspect in any entrepreneurial environment. You will never be able to convince the undistinguished entrepreneur to look at something new and help him or her see a compelling reason to be an early adopter if you are not fully convinced yourself.

And, moreover, the undistinguished entrepreneur does not know as much as you do. You are the subject-matter expert. You live with projects, clients, and their issues; the undistinguished entrepreneur does not.

You can also look into global issues that are being met with new technologies. Some of the new global issues that attracted Rajiv's attention pertained to renewable energy, clean water, and green initiatives, among others. Rajiv saw that the IT industry in India was examining its own use of natural resources. Infosys, India's leading IT firm, formulated a unique green IT implementation that focused on energy savings and reduction of carbon footprint. Tata and Reliance, two other leading Indian firms, also started on a number of green initiatives.

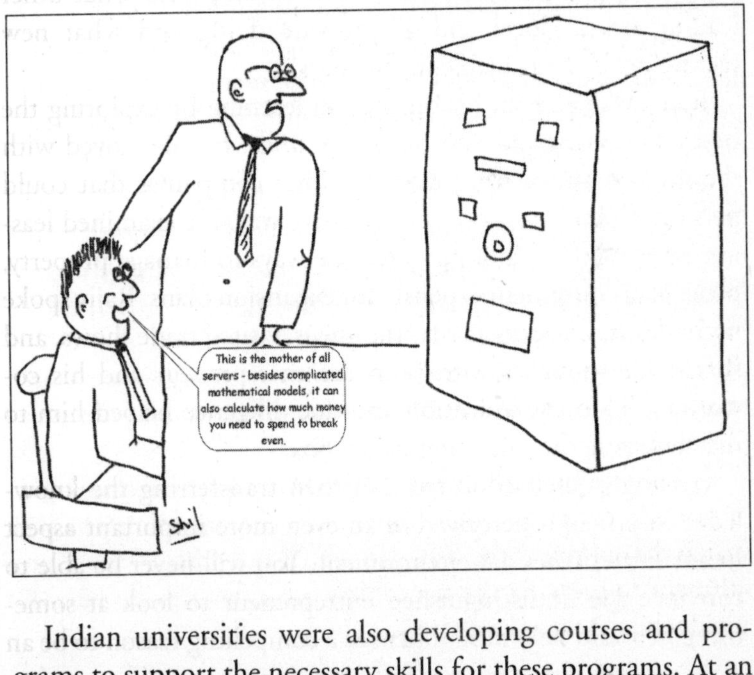

Indian universities were also developing courses and programs to support the necessary skills for these programs. At an entrepreneurship summit at the Delhi Technological University

(DTU) that Rajiv went to, he saw that there was a strong emphasis being laid on growing green enterprises and providing the training programs necessary for that effort. Rajiv heard the head of DTU, P.B. Sharma, speak about the new-age entrepreneurs, who, besides protecting interest of man and nature, will also achieve the highest level of quality and productivity.[15]

The prestigious Indian School of Business[16] (ISB), Hyderabad, Indian Institutes of Technology (IIT), and Indian Institutes of Management (IIM) have also been promoting and providing training not only for the green industry but also for organic socioeconomic growth, thus creating opportunities for entrepreneurs. Similarly, leading institutions in other countries have been building awareness and providing training to direct energies along paths that yield both environmental benefits to the communities and business opportunities to the socially connected entrepreneurs.

Jeffrey Pfeffer at Stanford Graduate School of Business has explained how training has conventionally been considered to benefit largely in the long term.[17] As the costs of training are immediate, many companies avoid the expense by not providing it. Thus, companies that do make training a high priority, gain a competitive advantage by building strong cultures and retaining highly skilled employees who contribute to their further successes.

By helping to educate your coworkers on new technologies or procedures or even what competing firms are doing, you will enrich the culture at the firm and which also reflects your commitment to growing the firm. Here are a few tips on what to avoid while sharing knowledge:

- Inundating the undistinguished entrepreneur with too much technical information in the hope that it will convince him or her to agree with what you have to say

- Becoming a self-proclaimed "expert" in a skill area
- Believing and acting as if nobody but you could have the same command over your subject
- Assuming that all your ideas are failure-proof and that the undistinguished entrepreneur should follow them without questioning you

18

If you were in the undistinguished entrepreneur's shoes

IF you ever get a chance to sit in the entrepreneur's chair, perhaps it will help you understand how the world looks from his or her perspective. Sitting there will also compel you to ask yourself what the undistinguished entrepreneur keeps thinking, why there is shouting instead of decisions, and why the entrepreneur is obsessed with bringing in more revenue instead of planning how to do so.

You are also likely to notice that the world is not that green from the top. Keeping the revenues flowing and being able to meet sustainability requirements and customer demands are not easy tasks. The constant stress of declining project orders eats away at the entrepreneur's time and energy. Add to that the fact that the products and services that the company offers may not be keeping the competition at bay and you will see that it is not easy for the undistinguished entrepreneur to be calm and composed. Changing competitors, noncompliant vendors, and a general climate of business uncertainty make the undistinguished entrepreneur's work no easier. If you know what he or she is trying to accomplish, you will have a better understanding of how you fit in.

That brings us to the two most important things an entrepreneur needs for success—a vision and a charted path toward the vision. Everything else follows.

Entrepreneurs are often dreamers and analyzers at the same time. In other words, there is a creative–emotive side and a practical–pragmatic side. Typically, an undistinguished entrepreneur does not balance these two very well. That is where you come in. If you are planning to learn the rules of entrepreneurship from the undistinguished entrepreneur and at the same time gain his or her trust and gain visibility of everything (that the undistinguished entrepreneur sees), you have to look at the financial side of sustainability.

Herbert N. Woodward, president of International Science Industries Inc, emphasizes the importance of making a firm financially sound.[18] He points out that sales growth should not be seen as true growth. Several firms have used marginal income accounting (not considering overhead in the cost of manufacturing a new product) or breakeven accounting (assuming overhead to be fixed, for the most part). These practices give

a false sense of success. Unsound cost accounting and misallocation of overhead to some other product or service line is a common financial pitfall for small businesses.

Even if the undistinguished entrepreneur is happy about the growing revenue, hidden costs can be eating away at the profits. Woodward suggests keeping a running tab on the balance sheet and getting as much cash as possible from accounts receivable, inventory, and accounts payable.

John O. Whitney, speaking at Columbia University's Graduate School of Business, emphasized the importance of cash in keeping any business competitive.[19] Whitney suggests that it is also very important to make all information easily accessible to the CEO, help him or her develop strong connections with vendors and suppliers, and reduce layers of management to increase visibility and accessibility.

Procedural Lessons

JEFF Wilke, senior executive at Amazon.com, while speaking at an event at Anderson School, UCLA, explained how strong operations management has been Amazon's chief competitive advantage.[20] Wilke discussed some of the advanced operations research techniques that Amazon uses to optimize its supply chain. Wilke also mentioned that Amazon's operational performance has improved markedly over its history and has allowed Amazon to grow its sales at a high rate while not having to invest in new distribution facilities. This efficiency has enabled Amazon to not only sustain but also prosper in an industry littered with dot-com blowouts.

In the Procedural Section, we looked at some of these basic tenets for improving the SF (remember Sustenance Factor), implementing operational controls and increasing efficiency within the undistinguished enterprise.

We learned how to:

- Build discipline within the firm (early to work, caution regarding pet peeves, minimal chattiness, no asking of favors)
- Implement project management methods (be proactive, keep schedules visible, be assertive in communication)
- Establish and support strong teamwork (positive feedback, sharing of knowledge, and participation in social sports)

- Instill professionalism (no "bypassing," no personal use of office resources, no expensive gifts, use of scrub savers)
- Gain knowledge about the firm (stand in the undistinguished entrepreneur's shoes, manage activities at work, set employer expectations)

The preceding list presents examples of how you can better manage the activities at the firm, but it hits only the highlights: discipline, project management, teamwork, professionalism, and knowledge in establishing procedural controls. Juan Lopez, Rajiv Sinha, and Linh Chun, all tried to promote these activities by developing procedures within their organizations, without the use of extra resources.

As you define procedures, you can run valuations of the firm, look for economies of scale and scope, consider reengineering where needed, identify critical success factors, check the financials to identify faulty practices and look for ways to change them, and consider how you can learn and train others about the industry and its best practices.

You should also look out for red flags, such as practices that reduce profitability levels, dependence on a limited number of product lines, and a declining current ratio (ratio of current assets to current liabilities, which measures a company's ability to pay short-term obligations). Even where this analysis is not a crisis-management exercise, it is a good opportunity for you to take a deeper look at the undistinguished entrepreneurial firm and help the entrepreneur in establishing leverage and controls for managing growth.

Once the undistinguished entrepreneur has implemented these controls, the next task is to establish a culture at the undistinguished firm that will support effective and high-functioning human behaviors. These behavioral ways are discussed in the next section.

■

Procedural Clinic

IN the procedural clinic, we will help two entrepreneurs who have come to us to ask for help.

Entrepreneur 1: The East Indian grocery-store chain

> The first entrepreneur owns a chain of East Indian grocery stores in Southern California. He wants to build a warehouse and centralize his inventory as he feels that doing so would save a lot on logistics and enable him to get higher discounts from wholesalers. Also, he knows that using an obsolete system can kill his profits. But nothing much is changing. His accounting and inventory systems have been victims of the "Trojan" virus, the effect of which is inactivity.
>
> The undistinguished entrepreneur trusts only one employee in every store. The employees do not get along well with one another, so there is not much information sharing among them.
>
> The entrepreneur is not sure of what he wants and seems to have no goals for growing or managing the stores.
>
> What changes should this undistinguished entrepreneur make?

Entrepreneur 2: The data-entry firm

The second entrepreneur's firm is in New Jersey. His customers are primarily lawyers and doctors. A year-and-a-half ago, he outsourced some of the data-entry work to a firm in Hong Kong. However, he has noticed that he is losing control over product quality. Even though he has a quality-assurance team, the team is not catching all the problems. What he has now is an inbox full of complaints from the clients.

He is thinking of eliminating the offshore connection and doing all the data entry in-house. At the same time, he thinks the quality assurance team in New Jersey is not doing a good job of oversight. There is a lack of schedule visibility and little interaction between the offices.

As per the contract, the Hong Kong partner initiates work only after receiving a 50 percent advance payment on each project, with the remaining 50 percent coming when the project is completed.

How would you bring more control to the data-entry entrepreneur?

■

Behavioral Ways

To build discipline and instill culture within the entrepreneurial firm

RICHARD GIORLA, owner of the famous [illegible]
in Studio City, Southern California, [illegible]
transaction [illegible]
that till he learned [illegible]
venture. [illegible]
antly, [illegible]
there [illegible]
Now, [illegible]
concern [illegible]
and so is [illegible]

Tracking [illegible]
all do [illegible]
that area, [illegible]
improve [illegible]
disting[illegible]
let you know [illegible]
others. [illegible]
he or she [illegible]
situations and [illegible]
to theirs.

Learning [illegible]
external [illegible]
your resources [illegible]
you to handle [illegible]
or her to [illegible]
with the team.

Besides tracking [illegible]
guished enterprise, [illegible]
the [illegible]

RICHARD GIORLA, owner of the famous Cardio Barre fitness in Studio City, Southern California, tracks all details of every transaction made.[21] He hadn't realized the importance of that till he learned some lessons at his previous coffee-shop venture. Due to lack of internal controls and, more importantly, absence of ethics within the culture, an employee there regularly handed out freebies when Richard was out. Now, Richard's mother handles the finances at the fitness concern and all the details go through her. Business is great and so is the accountability!

Tracking behavior of others around us is something we all do subconsciously. If we can build more discipline in that area, we will not only be alert for changes but also improve our behavior-forecasting ability. Tracking the undistinguished entrepreneur's behavior over time will also let you know what criteria he or she uses to label you and others. The entrepreneur's reaction might depend on how he or she has observed the way others react in various situations and how your behavior stacks up in comparison to theirs.

Learning some of the ways the entrepreneur reacts to an external stimulus (a loss, for example) will help you tailor your responses and reactions. In addition, that will enable you to handle the entrepreneur's mood swings and get him or her to listen to problems, react calmly, and craft solutions with the team.

Besides tracking behavior of everyone at the undistinguished enterprise, you have to also establish a culture at the undistinguished firm that can support effective and high-functioning human behavior and instill positivity in the firm. For that, you have to:

- Consider the undistinguished entrepreneur's personality. Does he or she trust anyone? Has he or she been duped in the past? What about creativity? Ethics? Emotional expression? Conduct in regard to finances?
- Study the firm's existing culture. What are the knowledge-sharing practices? What are the standards of performance and accountability? How customer-friendly is the firm? How employee-friendly is the workplace? What do employees wear to work? What are their educational backgrounds and industry experiences?
- Look at the pool of employee skills and consider what each employee or employee group thinks of the undistinguished entrepreneur. Do employees see their jobs and roles in the company in a positive way?

■

19

You are what you wear

EVERY morning, Mark Gordon heard the alarm, snoozed, turned off the second alarm, and then slept in. To help him get started, he bought a programmable coffee machine and set it to make coffee early, but that didn't help either. Mark's problem was not due to sleep deficit or any sleep disorder but due to a complete lack of motivation at work. Gradually, that lack of motivation started to reflect in Mark's attitude and work, and, finally, in the way he dressed and carried himself.

Mark got the shock of his life when he was summoned by the entrepreneur for a one-on-one. The entrepreneur showed Mark e-mails from three clients who had complained about the firm's lack of professionalism. In two of the e-mails, Mark's inappropriate dressing was also brought to the entrepreneur's attention.

If you don't want to repeat Mark's story, gear your dress to making others comfortable and avoiding expression of aggression or anger. A smartly dressed person is considered more amicable not only by clients but also by team members and the entrepreneur. It is important—and smart—to build a decent wardrobe for yourself.

Use clothes that fit you well and maintain the decorum and dignity of the profession. They go a long way in silencing opposition to your ideas, including opposition from the undistinguished entrepreneur, who will realize that you consider your job very important.

Before you change your wardrobe, find out how much freedom you have in dressing for work. In most professions, business-casual clothing is appropriate, but if you have a meeting with a client or some event outside the firm, dress formally. Never dress too casually, even on casual Fridays. Distressed jeans will only cause distress! It is better to err on the formal side than to be overly clubby and undermine your good image. All it takes is one occasion for the undistinguished entrepreneur to observe and take note of your bad taste—and that repressed opinion can come out the next time you ask for a new marketing campaign budget.

Browse your wardrobe every now and then. Fads keep changing but you can stick to some basic styles. Choice of colors, designs, and fabric also goes a long way in giving you a sharp look. Subscribe to fashion magazines and follow style-focused internet sites and TV programs.

At the same time, keep your eyes open for clearance sales on major brands on the internet or at retail stores. You can make yourself a "friend of the trend" and still keep your bank account intact.

20

Start saying no

GEORGE THOMPSON was a nice guy. With a rock-solid mechanical engineering background and numerous patents to his credit, he was considered a sharp mind in his field in the auto industry in Michigan. However, with a growing family and payments on a palatial house that he bought during the real-estate boom, he had begun to feel the brunt of the changing economy. As a result, working for the undistinguished entrepreneur became almost enslavement. He would go out of his way (literally, as well as figuratively) to accommodate all the entrepreneur's demands.

In time, George noticed that the more he complied with those demands, the more he was taken for granted. He thought he would do better by leaving the firm. He started looking for a job, only to be turned down repeatedly. He then decided to change the way he presented himself; and when he did, he discovered a completely different side of the entrepreneur.

You might have thought of leaving the undistinguished entrepreneur too. Then you probably thought some more and decided that the current economy might not be so good a time to give up a job. So you decided to stay and put up with the demands, reasonable or not.

Respect engenders respect. But the undistinguished entrepreneur never gets the fact that every time he or she insults and hurts you, it increases the chances of your negative reaction. The undistinguished entrepreneur also fails to understand that some collective decisions will go against his or her wishes. Your first step is to practice saying *no*, or if that seems too harsh, try saying: "Let me think about it." If even that seems undoable, perhaps you might need assertiveness training as you might be suffering from the Chronic Yes-man Syndrome (CYS).

It is understandable that you may not want to appear confrontational, and there are several situations in which it's very hard to say *no*. For example, one where you've been asked to take on a higher level of responsibility, beyond your normal tasks. Another is when you have reason to think that saying *no* will halt or hinder your advancement.

Under such situations, you may want to consider the following rules of engagement:

- Decline wisely and respectfully so that the undistinguished entrepreneur does not take your refusal personally.
- In a polite private conversation, ask for the opportunity to let the situation work itself out naturally. Tell the entrepreneur that your goal is to instill professionalism in the culture of the firm and ask him or her to refrain from belittling you in front of others.
- If the undistinguished entrepreneur objects to your idea, say nothing and listen until he or she stops talking. Summarize what was said, then suggest a direction to take and propose the next action steps.

This might also be the right time for us to talk about the negotiation skills you have in your bag of tricks (those that you've been saving for requesting a salary raise). In the world of negotiations, everything boils down to two negotiating approaches: distributive bargaining, where one loses and the other wins; and integrative bargaining, where both parties win (which is possibly how the phrase "win–win" came about).

Perhaps, the entrepreneur has always opted for distributive bargaining to ensure that he or she wins all the time. However, if the undistinguished entrepreneur is told that there is an integrative way of doing things and that outcomes are longer lasting, there might be a positive response. Show the entrepreneur that the pie that he or she is trying to divide can be grown to serve every party involved and that your primary interests are not necessarily opposed to his or hers. The entrepreneur wants a successful firm. You want a great career. You and the entrepreneur can align your goals and come to a middle path where there is a win–win dynamic.

21

Take criticism constructively

IN addition to not dressing appropriately, Mark Gordon had another problem: he did not take criticism well. When the entrepreneur brought out the clients' e-mails criticizing Mark's lack of professionalism, Mark became defensive instead of listening. Mark gave examples (and justification) of why he was right in behaving the way he did and why he reproached the clients. Next, Mark started blaming his coworkers. He even questioned the credibility of the entrepreneur.

Mark was let go a month later. He could have found a much better way to prove his point. What Mark did not know was how to separate personal ego from business activities. He didn't know how to demonstrate professionalism.

Each time the entrepreneur makes an unsolicited comment on how to do things differently, there is a good chance that he might have seen success in the past while doing it that way. Control your impulses and see the criticism as an opportunity to work together on a development plan. Take the advice and learn "the right way" of doing it.

Time and again, he or she can get on your nerves, almost provoking you to a fight. If the undistinguished entrepreneur makes a personal attack, do not respond emotionally. Reacting makes you an easy target for more personal attacks.

Evaluate the risks involved in responding to criticism—the reasoning in your rebuttal has to be very effective. Do not say anything to cast doubt on the undistinguished entrepreneur's qualifications, as that will not help to promote your stand on the issue at hand and will just provoke more emotional responses and expressions of frustration.

Here are a few pointers for responding to the undistinguished entrepreneur's criticism:

- Make a reply that sets the stage for further conversation.
- Make a brief statement so that he or she asks you to repeat or elaborate.
- Focus on the facts. Discuss why, where, and what.
- Conclude the meeting on a positive note.

Some criticisms are just plain hard to take; they can be debilitating as well as insulting. However, the sooner you can express how you feel about any public humiliation, the better it is for you.

What you should avoid at all cost is being typecast.[22] Nobel laureate Daniel Kahneman and Amos Tversky have shown how humans estimate a quantity by starting from an initial value or notion and adjusting it to arrive at an answer or conclusion. They call this anchoring and adjustment, and they have demonstrated that the final result can be wrong if the initial anchoring value is wrong, even after all the best-intentioned adjustments.

So, it is important that you set your own initial anchor value at the level you want with the entrepreneur. Otherwise, no matter how many adjustments you make later, it will not necessarily change your image.

22

Learn to deal with possible attention deficit disorder

DAVID HANSEN, the IT entrepreneur from Orange County, was always thinking; he was perpetually occupied with one thought after another. He was thinking of suppliers, customers, technologies, employees, bills, cost-cutting, cash flow, paychecks, and accounts, just to give a partial list. As a result, he often missed the big picture and ended up playing catch-up. In David's case, this condition might have just come bundled with entrepreneurship but his behavior would probably draw the attention of anyone who knows what attention deficit disorder (ADD) looks like.

A good number of entrepreneurs are like David in the way their thoughts run from one thing to another. The undistinguished entrepreneur has multiple ideas at the same time, but not multiple successful ideas; is full of energy, but has problems focusing and prioritizing. Although research is still underway, experts are noticing that entrepreneurs are increasingly falling prey to ADD (the hyperactive type or the inattentive type). Dr Kathy J. Marshack's ADD Entrepreneurs Research Project has gathered numerous such experiences, which are posted on her website (www.kmarshack.com).[23]

The undistinguished entrepreneur might have problems holding on to success. He or she might make a fortune but then lose it all. Restlessness conflicts with a strong commitment to follow through. So the undistinguished entrepreneur ends up disappointing partners, investors, customers, employees, and even family members.

When the undistinguished entrepreneur asks you about anything that you are working on, you can expect another question to come flying your way, even before you start responding to the first. So keep your responses short, whether or not the entrepreneur has attention deficit (hyperactivity) disorder.

Here are some **CARE** tips to help you manage the entrepreneur who shows signs of an ADD:

1. **C**urb his perfectionism—ask him to focus on strengths.
2. **A**sk the undistinguished entrepreneur to structure his thoughts—set boundaries and goals.
3. **R**equest his undivided focus on tasks.
4. **E**ase the undistinguished entrepreneur's anger and regulate his or her energy.

Have the invoices gone out? Are you working the phones? Who went to pick Jim up from the airport?

23

Manage the undistinguished entrepreneur's "I want this now" attitude

ALONG with a preoccupation with multiple thoughts, David Hansen of Orange County, California, also had a habit of becoming anxious and disturbed at the slightest issue that came up at his IT firm. David believed that if something was on his mind, it had to be treated with utmost urgency, whether it was important or not. For him, the firm was still a one-man shop and all the employees were his extensions. For his employees, controlling David's dictatorial behavior was next to impossible.

Undistinguished entrepreneurs like David can tell you to drop everything and work on Project A, and then, a half hour later, demand reasons as to why you have not been working on Project B. For some entrepreneurs, the typical frame of mind is that *everything* is urgent. Situations like this show how unclear some of their goals are. Worse, this attitude leaves room for irrational escalation of any issue any time.

The problem is not due to a real situation of increasing urgency. Not only does the undistinguished entrepreneur repeatedly put you under a mixed spell of panic and confusion, but he or she can also be extremely rude when you try to get instructions on prioritizing.

To combat this situation (and perhaps instill patience in the undistinguished entrepreneur), you can try the following strategies:

- When a project is assigned to you or your team, set up a tracking system or obtain some documentation from the undistinguished entrepreneur in case he or she changes priorities. The purpose is to record any variance.
- Be pleasant, willing, and patient when asked to do something but apprise the undistinguished entrepreneur of your current workload and priorities.
- Share the big picture. Explain how all projects could be done faster and have a positive impact on the bottom line, if reprioritizing is minimized.
- To defuse the situation. Ask the undistinguished entrepreneur for his or her input in a completely unrelated area. This may help to relieve the sense of urgency and preoccupation.

24

Organize the undistinguished entrepreneur's work

ACCORDING to management guru Peter Drucker, your success depends not only on how well you do your job but also on how well your supervisor does his or hers. And that means you must become adept not only at managing your work, but also at knowing how the undistinguished entrepreneur manages his or hers.

Rajiv Sinha was trying not only to assess the situation in the Delhi-based textile company, but also to bring more structure into its operations. Rajiv followed Drucker's philosophy and spelled out not only his own goals and objectives, but also those of the entrepreneur.[24] Rajiv delegated work to various departments as well as to the entrepreneur.

Undistinguished entrepreneurs focus most on past achievements and on imitating (or copying) other market leaders instead of thinking about new market entries or innovative product strategies. A large portion of their entrepreneurial time is also spent in gathering internal intelligence and watching employees.

It would be wise to give the entrepreneur ways to improve his or her throughput (and subsequently yours). Arrange a meeting with a strategic partner or a client. Create easy-to-understand reports on new industries, new products, and different ways to promote and deliver existing products for the undistinguished entrepreneur. Such activities will give the undistinguished entrepreneur some envisioning work to do and help him examine the options and avenues for growth. These big picture activities will also save the employees from excessive scrutiny and take the company beyond the Success stage (or stage 3 that we had discussed earlier).

25

Congratulate the entrepreneur!

VINOD KHOSLA says: *"Entrepreneurship is about those who dare to dream the dreams and are foolish enough to try and make their dreams come true."*

When Natasha Anderson started Emerald Frozen Yogurt, it was a small fish in the big frozen-dessert market. Natasha was health conscious and a strong proponent of organic food (as were many of her Silicon Valley neighbors); so she decided to bootstrap and pull together resources to open a couple of shops in an area not served by the frozen yogurt chains. She did the math, studied the industry extensively (using Porter's 5 Forces framework, among others), conducted due diligence on 3Cs and 4Ps of similar firms, worked the net present value calculations, and designed a business plan.

With a high burn rate, she went through all her reserves in just six months. Not discouraged, she pitched her ideas to angel investors and gave up a large equity for a very small amount of money, just to keep running. She added more employees, and with them came their innovative ideas. Finally, she saw the light at the end of the tunnel when her books showed her emergence from the red. And the rest, as they say, is history.

Almost every entrepreneur has been a risk-taker and a maverick in his or her approach. Another such example is FedEx's Fred Smith.

FedEx's Fred Smith wrote a term paper when he was at Yale on how underserved the market for a timely and efficient package delivery system was, and he received a "C" grade on that. Fred Smith, however, remained convinced that there was a large untapped market, and after struggling for the first few years and being close to bankruptcy more than once, he finally took his idea to fruition. In 1973, FedEx was started as a service company with values such as 100 percent guarantee, computerized tracking, ownership of planes, and a high commitment to employees. All these important values helped define FedEx's culture and helped it grow and sustain that. In 1998, FedEx achieved a 50 percent share of the overnight mail and package delivery market.[25]

Needless to say, a lot of these risk-taking entrepreneurs have done a few things right, which is why you work for him or her (and not the other way around). Congratulating the undistinguished entrepreneur (for even small things) is a great practice and helps open channels of communication. The entrepreneur's thoughts can have merit, so he or she deserves a praise every once in a while.

Here are a few suggestions for offering congratulations without sounding too flattering:

- Determine what mood the entrepreneur is in. If he or she is busy, angry, or otherwise distracted, it might be better to pick another time.
- Study the cause for congratulating him or her, even just a little. If the undistinguished entrepreneur has won a contract as a result of a lot of effort, find out more about it. If the undistinguished entrepreneur's son made it to the local high school football team, try to find something positive to say about the team's record.
- Do not drift away from the topic and refer to things that are too personal.
- If congratulating the entrepreneur calls for a nice card, go out and buy one.

Let the undistinguished entrepreneur know about your successes and contribution to the entrepreneur's successes as well. You can slip this in while congratulating and perhaps earn some praise for yourself. After all, strategies can come from within the firm.

"An entrepreneur crafts strategy perpetually," according to Henry Mintzberg of McGill University and entrepreneurs constantly search for emergent strategies in the patterns of the workplace.[26] So, if you give some ideas and past success stories to the entrepreneur while passing the congratulatory note, it can help the entrepreneur build the organization further on those tested ideas.

26

Socialize, but don't be overly sociable

OFFICE socializing helps people to work as a team. At an entrepreneurial firm, you will never achieve your full potential unless you socialize because socializing helps you position yourself so that others are aware of your skills, your dedication, and the ways you can contribute to the growth of your team and your company.

Take the time to attend company gatherings because they provide opportunities to hobnob with decision makers (aside from the undistinguished entrepreneur) and get to know them in a broader context. Talking to them about both work and non-work-related topics will help develop camaraderie.

Good managers, with social skills, are also great relationship experts and operate as focal points where they manage conflicts as well as look after the interests of the units. While socializing and networking is good, keep some limits or you may unknowingly enter the over-socializing zone. Too much socializing suggests that you are gossiping, escaping from work, or behaving in an overly familiar way.

Jim Rose, from our earlier example of the bookstore, maintained a large group of friends at work. At the store, he talked with them constantly about pretty much anything—how his cat behaved when he was sick, how his mother saved money by using coupons, why he would not call women he had met in the elevator, and why he liked eating hamburgers at 2 o'clock in the morning. Even the people browsing for books at the store could hear him. He would even ask many of his coworkers and customers out on dates. Several customers chose not to come back to the store because of Jim's conduct.

With the likes of Jim in mind, it is best to establish a few ground rules if you would like to socialize without alarming your fellow employees or the undistinguished entrepreneur, who may see your chatting as a pointer that you don't have enough work to do.

- Keep some distance from your chatty coworkers and maintain a professional and positive work atmosphere.
- Bring excessive socializing to the attention of others as they may slip into it without realizing it. Call a meeting or send an e-mail suggesting that too much socializing can potentially reduce productivity and delay the deliverables.
- Let your colleagues know they should not take frequent 15-minute coffee breaks.

- Keep your friendships outside the workplace. When going out with coworkers, do not talk about issues that should stay in the office and do not make that an event for complaining about the entrepreneur.
- Discourage your work friends from stopping by your office too frequently, for non-work-related discussions.

27

Control flights of fancy

AFTER trade school, Ed Nguyen spent five years with the prototyping team at an entrepreneurial firm that manufactured plastic collectibles. Ed worked closely with the entrepreneur and under his direction, created product prototypes. The entrepreneur was supposed to review the prototypes and identify the feasibility vis-à-vis costs and production setup. In other words, the entrepreneur was the one to give the product the final Yay or Nay. However, it wasn't that easy. The undistinguished entrepreneur would come up with more and more ideas and never settle on one. Disappointed, Ed once commented that the entrepreneur had too many ideas and too few that hit the mark.

The creativity that stirs and supports an entrepreneurial firm can stray too far from feasible product design at times. Creativity needs research, direction, and motivation to make it valuable and viable. It is very easy for the undistinguished entrepreneur to get excited and become overly optimistic. It is your job to bring him or her down to reality, get the facts across, and save the firm from a possibly disastrous venture.

Guy Kawasaki of Garage Ventures stressed the importance of getting into products that have a high degree of uniqueness and high value to customers.[27] But an entrepreneur should never spend too much time perfecting a product. Instead, he or she should take the product to market and churn out successive versions so as not to miss any possible opportunity.

When the undistinguished entrepreneur starts thinking, he or she is often immediately creative. The undistinguished entrepreneur scribbles and writes and browses the web, and doesn't stay in one spot long enough to work on any one area worth exploring. This goes on until he or she remembers one of the other 200 things still to be done. Lack of creativity is not so

much an absence of the ability to create as it is a lack of focus and discipline. If ever on the lookout for new ideas, the undistinguished entrepreneur may even borrow ideas from others and use them without permission.

According to psychoanalyst Silvano Arieti, it takes quite a few different qualities and practices to be creative, and to sustain creativity.[28] These include daydreaming, freethinking, readiness to catch on to similarities, replaying of past conflicts, alertness, and, most importantly, discipline. I am assured that quite a few of these are already being practiced by the undistinguished entrepreneur near you.

However, creativity might not always involve creating a service or product from scratch. According to Henry Mintzberg at McGill University, the entrepreneur's creativity and strategy are driven by corporate capabilities gained in the past and foreseeable market opportunities of the future.[29] Organizations look to keep their current strategies and practices in the name of stability but as an industry changes, the entrepreneur should seek out emergent strategies as well. There might be a different way of doing things—maybe more cost effective or more pleasing. Seeking out these strategies provides yet another important opportunity for the entrepreneur to be creative.

Supporting the undistinguished entrepreneur's ideas for new products is not a bad idea, even though a large majority of them might be difficult to implement. Look into the practical side of all new ideas—how they can be implemented, what would the costs be, and how easy it would be to sell a product that resulted from them. In other words, what are the chances of success?

You can help the undistinguished entrepreneur with a "go" or "no-go" decision on new ideas. The ideas can take any form or shape but you have to determine their feasibility and keep the undistinguished entrepreneur from flying too high.

Another way to help the undistinguished entrepreneur might be to find ways to take a second look at existing product or service lines and recommend enhancements. Herbert N. Woodward, president of International Science Industries, encourages entrepreneurs to question the need for new product lines and rethink existing ones.

Look at the sales volume of the products. Is it growing? Are the products profitable (you may discover that existing products have high overheads that are stunting the growth of the firm)? What are the gross margins (lower gross margins need higher operating efficiency)? What do customers think about the products? How much effort is the sales department putting in to sell the products (lower pricing, more promotions, promoting your firm as a one-stop shop)?

You can research the facts and present your data in ways that get the entrepreneur's creative ideas rolling in a practical, positive direction, thus controlling the flights of fancy.

28

Be pragmatic

ED NGUYEN, from the plastic-collectible manufacturing firm, took a lot of flak from the undistinguished entrepreneur for not understanding the designs that existed only in the entrepreneur's mind. The entrepreneur would often ask Ed: "Can't you use your commonsense?" After a few such incidents, Ed *did* use commonsense—he stopped being creative and enthusiastic and focused on doing what the entrepreneur asked. He was tired of sharing his creative ideas with the entrepreneur and getting lambasted each time.

An inevitable part of being an undistinguished entrepreneur is that some decisions involve interests that are close to heart. The undistinguished entrepreneur cannot control his or her anger and that can be a major hurdle to advancement. You, as a trusted employee, will have to watch for signals that tell you when that anger is about to become public. Do not stick to your gut feelings when the entrepreneur is racing through a whim cycle. Leave your emotions outside the office and be as practical as you can in your workplace decisions.

The undistinguished entrepreneur might have been left-brained in his or her more composed and level-headed non-entrepreneurial days, but with time, he or she has become more right-brained. Many decisions are not entirely rational, and even the most rational ones are affected by emotions—emotions such as fear, as Amitai Etzioni of George Washington University has noted.[30] Etzioni has demonstrated that wholly rational decisions are extremely difficult because they generally require more data than we can obtain.

Along with data to fight his fears, you may have to drive change between two warring factions: the undistinguished entrepreneur and the more pragmatic professionals. You will have to investigate and evaluate the different options to achieve as happy medium—the challenge there is to take your findings through to meaningful outcomes that can prove your point. So, work on ideas that can give you quick wins to demonstrate to others how well you have thought through the issues. The key lies in striking a balance between the right and the left sides of your brain.

Chip and Dan Heath, the bestselling authors of *Made to Stick* and *Switch: How to Change Things When Change Is Hard*, have studied how change can be implemented by aligning our rational and emotional sides.[31] If we can direct the rational side, motivate the emotional side, and shape the path, even the toughest change can be made significantly easier and implementable. Likewise, if we align the emotional entrepreneur and the pragmatic employees (you and others) with a common focus, we can make things work and the firm will grow out of its undistinguished realm. Both emotive and practical aspects are important for the success of a small business—a well-balanced team will churn out creative products and sound strategies to take the firm to the next level.

29

Learn from your mistakes

GEORGE THOMPSON, the nice guy with the patents in Michigan, did not understand the need to set benchmarks and follow professional guidelines to achieve them. He presented himself as someone who was at the mercy of the entrepreneur. And that indeed was how the entrepreneur saw him. Soon thereafter, George started monitoring his own behavior and recording his mistakes. He also started reading the owner's disposition and began coaching himself to be bold but affable to emotional leaders (as the owner). He saw himself transform gradually. He also noticed that with his changed ways, the entrepreneur had started taking him more seriously.

Fear of mistakes and failures can create obstacles in a natural progression and force you to operate at low levels of effectiveness. The ability to deal constructively with failure is a skill that you learn by treating them as opportunities for growth.

Our mistakes are always those that teach us the most. I used to think that as I evolved, I would make fewer mistakes. However, I continue to make mistakes, but with time I have learned to discover them sooner and repeat them less often, if at all. Most successful people start with mistakes and failures.

Here are a couple things you can learn from mistakes:

- **Cut your losses.**
  I have learned from my investment management days to cut losses at the earliest possibility and minimize the negative impact of mistakes. It is when you refuse to accept that you made a bad decision (due to your gut feeling) that the mistake becomes even more severe. Wishful thinking does not get you out of bad situations. So be positive but not unrealistically optimistic.
- **Identify your mistakes and mitigate the impact.**
  Identifying a mistake is half the battle won, and many employees at entrepreneurial firms do not even realize that when they make mistakes. Next, you should identify all the possible root causes of the mistake and spell out the ways to avoid the causes, in order to prevent it from happening again. Then you check all the downstream effects of your mistake and find effective ways of mitigating them.

Learning from mistakes becomes even more critical if your firm is launching a new product line or service as there is no history of earlier mistakes to learn from. So, everything has to be based on assumptions. An assumption can lead to either a failure or a success, but only after it is acted upon and systematically recorded as knowledge.

A team led by Rita Gunther McGrath of Columbia University's Graduate School of Business has shown that by using *discovery-driven planning*, this process of using assumptions can be significantly improved.[32] If you are launching a new service or product, there are some things you can learn from the past about your assumptions. You can work backward and go through the assumptions you have already made and assess them against mistakes from similar past situations.

Alex Andon, a Biology and Environmental Science graduate from Duke University, got fascinated with marine animals while free-diving through underwater tunnels in coral reefs.

As Alex's passion grew, he found that people loved watching jellyfish but did not have access to the necessary tanks (with special water-flow patterns) and food to display jellyfish in captivity. The creativity was in the design as the tanks and the filters had to be of a certain shape so that the delicate jellies wouldn't get stuck or sucked into the tubing. Alex had accumulated extensive experience in building aquariums for his own research projects in college.

Subsequently, Alex founded a firm called Jellyfish Art on a platform of cutting edge jellyfish husbandry techniques.[33] With creativity in building tanks, Alex had to look to the other aspects of business—in a discovery-driven planning mode. There was no existing knowledge base to tap as he was a first mover in this industry. With discovery-driven planning came putting those assumptions into action—and a lot of realizations—facts like jellyfish survive only in very low temperatures and they consume frozen food high in fatty acids. In addition, minimal orders were to be procured before approaching distributors. For a little while, Alex kept going out to the beaches in San Francisco and collecting jellies to take the business from the survival to the success stage. Finally, he contracted with a professional distributor of jellies to ship them in sealed plastic bags inside insulated shipping boxes. That was the take-off point for the business.

In sum, the more you use your knowledge from earlier mistakes, the better are your chances of reducing mistakes in the future. Mistakes, when viewed as opportunities, can only propel you toward being a successful employee with the undistinguished entrepreneur.

30

Admit mistakes and move on

MARK GORDON, the employee who was let go for his lack of professionalism, also had a problem of not admitting mistakes. Mark would pass the buck for any issue to others in the team. Blaming the client for his mistakes was his easiest and most frequent escape. Mark would also say: "I told you so," quite often, but when it came to taking the responsibility for a project disaster, he would shy away completely.

Everyone makes mistakes but admitting them (in a timely manner) can prevent you from getting slaughtered. This resonates with what one of my elementary schoolteachers used to say: "Be a phoenix—admit your mistakes and spring back into action."

In large corporations, employee mistakes can be passed on to "the system" and even to other coworkers. However, in smaller firms, they get detected easily, particularly when the undistinguished entrepreneur triangulates. So, if you've made a mistake, come clean and move on. The undistinguished entrepreneur will respect your frankness. Of course, there is a possibility that he or she might not even realize that you made an error, but why take a chance?

Admitting mistake shows honesty and maturity. It also brings out your respect for the entrepreneur. Blaming a coworker or the situation (issues with e-mail, bad weather, stress) sounds unprofessional and leads the undistinguished entrepreneur to think that you are not ready to take on increasing responsibility because you shy away from ownership. On the contrary, even if the mistake was not entirely your fault, taking full responsibility will convince the undistinguished entrepreneur that you are advancing in the firm and can lead others.

Along with admittance of mistakes, you should also provide resolutions to mitigate the repercussion of your mistakes. Suggest solutions and provide alternatives that show that you have carefully evaluated the damage and identified what will fix the problem.

The style and presentation are as important as the content. If you handle your admission in a professional manner, it will help you establish trust and credibility with the undistinguished entrepreneur and will see you grow in the firm.

31

Provide constructive feedback when you disagree

LINH CHUN, the transcriptionist turned elementary school teacher in the Shanghai suburb, produced a manual and helped to establish channels of communication for everyone. As a frontrunner for implementing change in the organization, she brought the entrepreneur and other employees into the same room to assess needs and discuss how they could be met. She conducted focus groups with parents and site visits to other schools and wrote a comprehensive report in which she assessed the gaps and made recommendations for bridging them.

Most of us are not inclined to give feedback to an undistinguished entrepreneur. We believe that if we disagree with the entrepreneur, we should say nothing at all. We may learn over time to disagree in a tactful way, but we are always apprehensive in feedback situations. As a result, we offer only positives; the absence of balance takes away from one's credibility.

A first step is to examine your attitude about giving feedback. Do you avoid giving criticism to the undistinguished entrepreneur because you are afraid of the reaction? Are you concerned that giving negative feedback will result in a setback to your career? If you have difficulty in giving negative feedback about a problem, remember that it is likely that you are not the only one who has or recognizes the same problem.

Here are some suggestions for offering feedback:

- Use illustrations and facts to support what you say.
- When you give feedback on a specific issue, offer a solution, even a partial one or a vision of one. It is not a good idea to give feedback without presenting some direction for improvement.
- Choose the right time. Avoid times when the undistinguished entrepreneur is preoccupied with firefighting other issues.
- Take a bullet for the cause. If you champion a cause and the undistinguished entrepreneur decides to help you, be ready to take a bullet if he or she gets a lot of pressure or blame.
- Be sure the messenger never gets shot. Be a conduit for the undistinguished entrepreneur by conducting meetings with key employees and getting their seal of approval before talking to the entrepreneur.
- Listen to the undistinguished entrepreneur's defense. There may be a good reason that he or she has been doing things in a certain way.
- Moderate your feedback. Even constructive feedback can become too direct. So, to soften that, you can e-mail a moderated and abbreviated version to the undistinguished entrepreneur before you talk in person.

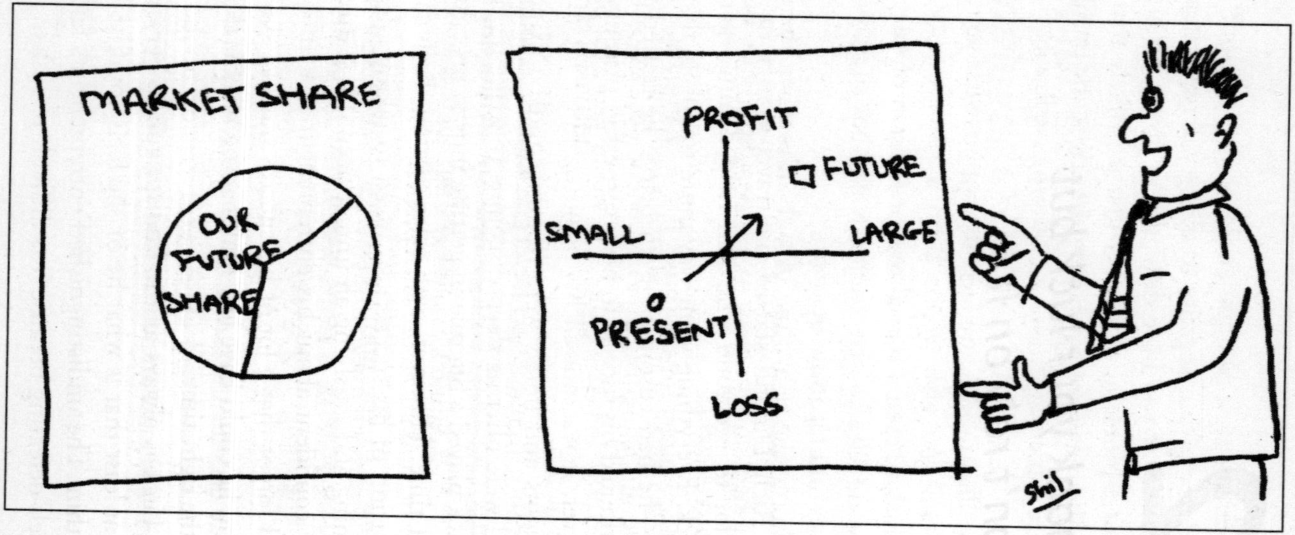

MARKET SHARE
OUR FUTURE SHARE
PROFIT
FUTURE
SMALL
LARGE
PRESENT
LOSS
Shil

32

Thank your luck but don't rely on it

WHEN Rich Durand started his travel agency in Paris, he owed a lot to everyone who had helped him—particularly, Lady Luck. Everything went way more smoothly than he had planned—he had customers even before he started the firm. Rich attributed his success to his greatness in planning.

However, it was not all his planning but a lot of luck. In truth, flights and hotels were running under capacity at the time and were offering deep discounts to make up the difference. Luck played a big role in getting him to his customers at the right time. However, with sales soaring, Rich forgot that a big portion of his success was owed to taking advantage of good timing and satisfying an unmet need. He started becoming over confident about his entrepreneurial acumen and his luck and forgot that a lot of his success was just sheer coincidence and he could have lost it all had he not hit the business path at the right time.

Lady Luck is always at the undistinguished entrepreneur's side, or at least that is what he or she feels comfortable about deep within. The undistinguished entrepreneur's faith in luck can be self-defeating because it is difficult to sustain a business by relying on luck alone. It takes hard work, research, calculated risk taking, and above all, timing, to sustain even good luck.

Not all successful entrepreneurs are competent, and not all failed ones are incompetent. Luck does play a part in success or failure, but luck favors the competent, hardworking entrepreneur. Louis Pasteur wrote that "*Chance favors the prepared mind,*" and Ernest Hemingway believed that each person makes his or her own luck. Samuel Goldwyn said: "*The harder I work, the luckier I get.*" Perhaps these views apply mostly to a successful entrepreneur and not so much to the undistinguished entrepreneur. The successful entrepreneur sees failure as a stepping stone to success and is aware that a streak of bad luck may yield or even make way for a brighter future. The successful entrepreneur also attracts "lucky" employees as he or she is interested in others' goals; and that results in even more "luck."

The undistinguished entrepreneur's false confidence in his or her ideas and luck as if *nothing can ever go wrong* can lead to unreasonable actions. The entrepreneur, with the aura of such overconfidence, refuses to listen to sensible suggestions, rejects any out-of-the-box pursuits, and does not hedge risks. Such blind faith gives the undistinguished entrepreneur the conviction that he or she can never err—so much so that a breakthrough idea may be greeted with mocking laughter rather than a decent hearing.

The undistinguished entrepreneur may have made some right assumptions in the past, such as focusing on the technical superiority of a product or promoting a certain way of delivery. Riding a wave of success, he or she may wrongly theorize that competitors will never be able to beat the firm's prices and products and miscalculate the sustainability of good luck. However, by pointing out how easily a few things could go against the undistinguished entrepreneur's assumptions, you can make the entrepreneur understand how rational decisions can help to offset some potentially bad outcomes and sustain the firm's success.

33

Turn the focus on the firm's culture

JUAN LOPEZ, at the engineering consulting firm, started his tasks by putting some controls in place, for example, project-management procedures and whiteboard techniques. However, he saw a broader issue: the need to boost employees' spirits and value their identities. He wanted to add the missing link that would make both employees and the entrepreneur proud of the firm and lead them to identify themselves with it. In other words, Juan wanted to instill a culture in the firm.

The undistinguished entrepreneur has always run away from the distant future and toward short-term goals. He (or she) has managed to keep the cash flow positive by contracting receivables and stretching payables. But this focus does not offer a means of establishing a strong culture.

Culture is a key enabler in improving practices and driving creative goals. Creativity and intellectual growth thrive in a culture with differences in views, backgrounds, and insights. A wide range of perspectives and contributions cultivates the ability of all employees to offer objective analyses and creates empathy within the entrepreneurial organization, so much so that it also impacts the bottom line of entrepreneurs.

Eric Flamholtz at UCLA's Anderson School of Management has assessed the impact of culture on firms' financial performance.[34] Flamholtz studied firms' existing cultures, looking at values such as the treatment of customers, treatment of employees, standards of performance and accountability, and found that the divisions that adhered to corporate culture saw greater profits than those that did not.

Getting the big picture, defining culture milestones, and instilling the right culture are fundamental to sustainability. In some firms, the entrepreneur is involved in numerous extra-curricular and teambuilding activities. Having such activities happen twice a week can seem slightly wasteful and somewhat irritating, but go along as these activities help to promote camaraderie and build a strong corporate culture.

34

Push for ethics in the organization

STEVE GAGRIN worked for a motel chain in a fiduciary role and knew everything about the business, but he was not happy with the way the owner treated him. Steve's wife was suffering from a terminal illness and in addition to caring for and worrying about her, he had to spend several hours at work to cover up for the entrepreneur's sketchy deals.

One day, while going over the accounts, the entrepreneur found gaps in the financials. The entrepreneur questioned Steve, only to find that Steve had been embezzling small amounts for the past several years. Steve, in his defense, told the entrepreneur how displeased he had been while working for the chain. He said that the main reason behind his loss of motivation and connection to his job was the entrepreneur's unethical and pushy dealings with the clients, partners, and employees.

An undistinguished entrepreneur tends to look for quick wins, even if he or she has to bypass ethical conduct and relationships for profitability.

Abraham Lincoln once said: "*Nearly all men can stand adversity, but if you want to test a man's character, give him power.*"

Ethical behavior begins with the founder or leader of the firm and is perhaps the single most important factor in how the firm functions. Business sustainability, working relationships, and credibility in the marketplace—all depend on ethics.

A firm's ethics constitute a code that helps an entrepreneur abide by rules and play fair. He or she should go beyond quick profitability by acting in an ethical manner toward partners, customers, and employees. From hospitals and auditors to telecommunication firms and energy companies, unethical behavior can be found everywhere. As we see public scandals unfolding one after the other, entrepreneurship programs in schools are still confused about ways to teach ethics. However, teaching remedial ethics at work would be a good solution to influence the culture positively and strengthen the ethical standards of the firm.

Ethics are based on values and not numbers, so knowing and acting on them can involve working around a thin subjective line.

We have all done something or the other that we could have handled more fairly or honestly or with greater benefit to others. But the key question is: "How ethical is ethical?"

As a simple measure of your ethics in business, examine how your conduct affects any of the following areas:

- Fairness
- Truth
- Relationships
- Conscience
- Outcome

35

Don't partake in politics

SAM COOPER, the self-proclaimed turnaround expert with the engineering consulting firm, introduced a divide-and-rule policy.

Despite his general unpopularity, Sam had formed a group of friends. He called them *homies* and was very courteous to them. At work, he talked with them about college football. By doing that, he established an informal secret society within the small firm. Sam would look after and help those who belonged to his society. What he did was lay the seeds of political conflict and chaos. Sam's successor, Juan Lopez, had to clear the air to reunite the firm's employees and get them to start thinking in terms of aligning their goals with the firm's.

Office politics is part of any job. And political conflict is based on differences in ideologies between groups. The sooner you know that, the better you'll be at surviving or thriving in the workplace.

Political conflict often takes root in groups that were formed initially to produce beneficial outcomes and there is nothing wrong with making friends at the office. People close in age may become friends, people in IT seek out other techies to discuss issues, the foodies experiment with new restaurants, and management trainees hangout together to discuss acquisition trends and market moves. Forming groups within the small organization is very beneficial and helps to create a vibrant culture, but carried too far, it can lead to the exclusion of others, hurt feelings, and engender bad morale.

Gossip goes hand-in-hand with office politics and it can hurt feelings and even disrupt careers. It supports and encourages coworkers who lie, take credit for work they did not do, and conduct themselves in other deceitful ways.

Here are a few rules you can follow to avoid getting embroiled in office politics:

- Keep a trail of all office communication.
- Make your accomplishments known, particularly if coworkers are unfairly trying to undermine your career.
- Don't let what others say demoralize you and affect your productivity in negative ways.
- Encourage open communication to understand your coworkers' perspectives.
- Take a lead in the resolution of differences so that the firm functions without a loss in motivation.

These tasks are difficult but the silver lining here is that the undistinguished entrepreneur will appreciate your jumping in to solve relationship crises and motivating everyone to work as a team.

Behavioral Lessons

MANY undistinguished entrepreneurs wrongly assume their organizations to have ample resources to continue to operate perpetually and thus see no need to bring *kaizen*—a Japanese term for efforts toward continuous improvement—into their management of the firm. In this section, we have learned the importance of adding the missing link—the human link—that is essential to sustaining the organization.

We have looked at a number of ways to influence the behavior of the entrepreneur and the employees.

- Track the undistinguished entrepreneur's behavior and manage his or her excesses—being overly emotional, letting the imagination fly out of control, an "I want this now" attitude, lack of organization in management including possible ADD, the conviction that luck is on one's side with slim evidence, a lack of understanding about the need of a culture.
- Manage your own behavior—congratulating the entrepreneur, admitting mistakes and moving on, learning from mistakes, taking criticism constructively, providing constructive feedback, saying *no* when necessary.
- Manage the firm's behavior—no politicking, set an example by dressing for success, avoiding over-socializing, driving ethics in the firm.

Again, this list is not exhaustive but it does point to problem categories that you should be alert to and informed about.

Once you have established some principles of the entrepreneurial organization's behavior, start looking at customer's behavior and changing priorities. Identify how they are changing and how should your firm change to attract and retain more customers.

You can begin looking for other red flags such as high burn rates, aimless investment in new products, reductions in customer orders, and employee turnover. You can do this by exploring the relationships between the undistinguished entrepreneur's vision and the strategies the enterprise applies by taking a closer look into how the organization plans and by tracking the direction in which the firm is heading.

These strategic ways are discussed in the next section.

■

Behavioral Clinic

LET us help a couple of entrepreneurs and learn something ourselves in the process.

Entrepreneur 3: The Spanish restaurant

Our third entrepreneur worked for many years at a strategy-consulting firm before he thought of living a laid-back life. He decided to open a Spanish restaurant in Orlando, Florida, to attract European tourists and expected that it would take off like crazy (something that many entrepreneurs expect but only a few experience). However, the sales were lukewarm to average, even though the economy was healthy at the time of the opening and tourists were arriving all the time.

The undistinguished entrepreneur is confused. Is there no market for Spanish food in Florida? He then started catering to the Latin American tourists by offering Mexican cuisines? Even that did not work.

His chefs, who were from both Spain and Mexico, never understood the way he behaved. He would review and question every intricacy of the kitchen with them. He even accused some of them of stealing from the cash register in his absence. He would never listen to their professional suggestions for improvements because he felt that the chefs and other employees were far beneath him.

How would you help this unhappy restaurant owner?

Entrepreneur 4: The magazine for women aged 25–40

The fourth entrepreneur has just started a woman's magazine. She intends the magazine to appeal to young professional women. She knew that brand and company culture were important for sales and for retaining talent, so she spent a lot of investor capital on promoting the brand. She even leased multiple floors of a building in downtown San Francisco so that she could display the magazine's name on the outside of the building.

Her main concern was that she was shorthanded. All the reporters and journalists juggled multiple tasks but were paid on a tight budget. As a result, they were losing motivation and there was a lot of procrastination and passing the buck.

There were also problems in delegation of tasks within the team. There was not a lot of discipline or innovation within the culture either. The entrepreneur was always preoccupied with multiple tasks and her job had become thankless. In addition, sales had not picked up the way she had forecasted.

How would you help this magazine owner?

■

Strategic Ways

To help you build the firm's future and put yourself and the firm ahead of the competition

ONCE you have defined procedures for operating the firm, achieved a reasonable amount of control in dealing with the entrepreneur's excesses and blind spots, and gained a solid understanding of how the firm should conduct business, you can look for ways to take the firm to a more professional level. This section focuses on identifying and applying some industry best practices to help the firm survive market ups and downs.

At this point, you should ask yourself some far-reaching questions about the entrepreneur and the firm.

- What are the undistinguished entrepreneur's goals for both the long and short term?
- Is the business profitable?
- Does the undistinguished entrepreneur have a roadmap or a strategic plan?
- How open is the entrepreneur to changes within the organization?
- How much awareness does the entrepreneur have about the industry and its market trends?
- Are customer preferences being addressed? Are they changing?
- What kind of information does the undistinguished entrepreneur need? How often? How detailed?

According to Sharon Bernstein of *The Los Angeles Times*, the most common small business pitfalls circle around not planning all aspects of the business.[35] The successful ones are those who learn from their mistakes and steady themselves.[36]

■

36

Focus on profitability, not sales

PROFITABILITY comes with increasing revenue and reducing cost. Most often, the entrepreneur knows about increasing revenues but needs to be reminded about cutting costs, increasing efficiency, and reallocating resources.

Natasha Anderson of Emerald Frozen Yogurt initially struggled with a high burn rate. Even with high revenues, the business was not profitable. She worked on cutting costs and designed procedures that could be learned and replicated easily. She implemented training programs for her staff and instilled a culture unique to her organization. Soon thereafter, the company started seeing better returns, but it was not until much later that it became profitable.

Most entrepreneurs start their own businesses because they have knowledge and experience in the industry. Not so many have business education; nor do they typically have a formal understanding of conducting business.

One of the first ways to help the entrepreneur is by working to lower the operating overhead in fixed-cost areas such as administration, wages, insurance, rent, and utilities. Even the owner's wages are a component of fixed cost. Look into project costs next and see whether the entrepreneur could obtain a higher return by using a younger employee base and introducing a strong training program. Instituting a robust employee incentive-rewards program could help to identify and motivate the cream of the crop and retain talent.

Alongside the effort to reduce overhead, you have to work on developing a strong marketing program to increase product sales. A solid marketing plan with high-quality products or services at attractive prices is the foundation for sales growth. Look into how the product has been meeting (or not meeting) the needs of the customer. Is there a customer segment the firm is missing out on? Is the market ready for another product or service (or an update of an existing product)? What are your competitors doing?

Do potential acquisition targets exist? What kind of brand awareness and image do you want to build?

Look at where you are planning to produce the product, the willingness of your customers to pay for the products or services, where and how you will sell the product, what discounts and promotions you can offer, and how you will distribute your products. To maximize profitability from sales, you have to ensure that marginal revenues equal marginal costs (Economics 101, as you might have read in your Xth standard economics book).

After reducing fixed overhead and establishing a strong marketing plan, you can look at three more areas to aid profitability: organization structure, policies for running the company, and the use of metrics.

- Build an organization chart that includes narratives. Define positions, roles, and responsibilities. The undistinguished entrepreneur should review the chart and determine why each position and role is necessary. How do the employees' wages and skills match up to their responsibilities?
- Define policies. Policies help the organization with the activities and tasks needed to execute ongoing responsibilities and promote the achievement of individual, team, and company goals. Policies lay the groundwork for procedures and also help build the culture of the firm.
- Identify the metrics you need and apply them. No execution procedure is complete without measurement. Metrics help the entrepreneur measure the difference between what profitability goals were and what was achieved.

37

Instill clarity in the organization's workflows

NATASHA ANDERSON interviewed 30 candidates before she hired Liz Abramsky to work with her. Liz had a venture capital background and expertise in establishing structure in portfolio firms. Liz's role in the venture capital company was to serve as an entrepreneur-in-residence at an ice cream company. Ice creams became her passion and she wanted to stay close to her passion. When Liz interviewed with Natasha, she did not have the remotest idea of what her position would entail. She took that as a challenge and laid out the roles for all employees, including her own. She also established a franchise plan. She worked on break-even analyses, pro forma income projections and cash flow tracking procedures, and laid out a detailed plan implementation schedule for Natasha to follow.

Not everyone at an entrepreneurial firm has a job description with well-defined expectations and responsibilities. Often, the company experiences delays and some buck-passing due to the absence or inadequacy of workflows.

The good news is that it is never too late to define, redefine, or refine workflows. John O. Whitney, while a visiting professor at Columbia University's Graduate School of Business, emphasized that the management should talk with each employee to disentangle and smooth out all work assignments.[37] Only after that should any redefinition or simplification of employee tasks be done.

Here are a few pointers to help you bring more clarity to workflows:

- If you have not been given a workflow chart or a list of expectations and responsibilities, draw one up. Document all responsibilities and roles.
- Incorporate paper forms into the workflows as the age-old method of directing forms from one department to another always works. After the paper format has brought more clarity in the flow of information, then move into enterprise-wide applications.
- Seek clarification when in doubt, without reflecting lack of depth or professional incompetence. Avoid repeatedly seeking out assistance at the earliest difficulty because doing so will become annoying and frustrating to the undistinguished entrepreneur.
- Watch out for challenges and obstacles in the assignment of tasks and try to foresee potential conflicts and problems during execution.
- Educate everyone to understand that there is nothing wrong with over-executing and under-promising.

In all of this, the most important underlying effort is to help the undistinguished entrepreneur see the big picture, manage change, and continuously work toward transparency. Transparency will motivate the undistinguished entrepreneur to do more and question less. Efforts to manage change and build credibility become successful when everyone contributes to the initiative, particularly the entrepreneur.

I am stuck in traffic ... I might be a little late
We are all waiting in the conference room...can you give us an ETA?
Shil

38

Understand long-term goals

AFTER Juan Lopez had established some procedures at the engineering consulting firm where he worked, he began efforts to instill culture. At the same time, he started reviewing where the firm was heading.

One Monday morning, Juan called a meeting of employees and the entrepreneur to discuss the firm's goals. What followed was a question–answer session that gave every employee the opportunity to envision collectively, along with the entrepreneur, where the company should go.

Opening one's own firm is often an entrepreneur's long-time goal, but the entrepreneur may not have applied a lot of thought and research to that effort. Through a series of trials and errors, the undistinguished entrepreneur got what he wanted or maybe more than that. With help from friends and family, the undistinguished entrepreneur made dreams a reality and became his or her own boss.

The key advantages of going entrepreneurial were many—the flexibility to set one's own hours, the opportunity to use one's expertise and creativity, and the end of taking direction from someone else. However, the disadvantages at some point outweighed the advantages. The undistinguished entrepreneur needed capital to start, uncertainties in revenues made planning difficult, and the entrepreneur was the sole sales generator as well as the chief operating officer.

For these reasons, it is highly likely that the undistinguished entrepreneur did not conduct a lot of due diligence during the initial planning and has probably been too busy or preoccupied to improve on the plan since then. This is where you come in.

We saw earlier that assumptions needed to be systematically changed into knowledge by discovery-driven planning, particularly when a firm enters a new industry.

This process of identifying long-term goals should also factor in looking out for opportunities that are amenable to expansion, diversification, integration; changing competitors, substitutes, new technology, more informed customers; sourcing and distribution layers; and, most importantly, determining whether current products or services are meeting customer needs. These are the questions that the entrepreneur should ask while refining the existing firm's business plan.

According to Adrian Slywotzky, this plan-refinement stage may also be the best possible time to evaluate the industry and changing customer preferences and consider a change in the business design.[38] Businesses that are in the value-growth phase can go into stagnation phase and finally become obsolete if they never change their business designs.

Your immediate job at this point is to search out the long-term goals of the entrepreneur. What does he or she want to do with the firm? Squeeze out profits and nothing more? Use it to achieve some other purpose? Reinvest in the firm and make it an industry powerhouse?

If the undistinguished entrepreneur is simply milking the firm for profits, sell the idea of growing the firm, acquiring other firms, or perhaps positioning the firm to be acquired. That way there is a good chance that the entrepreneur will reinvest, thus promoting *your* growth.

If the undistinguished entrepreneur is already working on growing the firm, help him or her identify what the key growth areas are. Research the industry, competitors, the current economic conditions, and budgetary constraints to address growth and make recommendations for sustainable progress.

39

Search out innovations and conduct research

INNOVATION is the mother of all revenue streams. After establishing a communication channel for all staff at her elementary school in the Shanghai suburb, Linh Chun took her efforts a notch higher and decided to implement some of the plans herself. She brought to the table an e-learning initiative to make it easier to offer elementary schooling to those in geographic areas with no elementary schools. She talked with her internet service providers, sought help from web designer friends of her husband, and then reworked the curriculum with a broader syllabus. Using low-budget marketing methods, she started spreading the word around. Very soon, the entrepreneur noticed a lot of interest in Linh's e-learning initiative.

Rajiv Sinha, at the textile manufacturing firm in New Delhi, was also smitten by the research-and-development bug. He wanted to know how much new cloth was being purchased every year by the target demographic. He sought out new markets within India and the world, identifying income levels, age groups, and cultural preferences. He studied customer preferences for ready-to-wear clothing versus custom-tailored clothing, and subsequently, the market for fabric by the yard. He already knew that in India, there had always been a high demand for just the fabric because most people preferred custom-tailored clothes. However, he recognized that customer preferences in India were changing; so he sought ways to introduce and market ready-to-wear dresses.

Rajiv also explored the idea of outsourcing knitting and sewing to countries with a lot of underutilized sewing skills that were available at an inexpensive price. After several meetings with the entrepreneur on the feasibility of the new product, Rajiv finally convinced the entrepreneur to go ahead with readymade garments for a pilot market. The new product line was a great success, with a large positive impact on the bottom line, for the entrepreneur.

Employees' research efforts show the entrepreneur that they are interested in increasing the bottom line and enabling the entrepreneur to spread his or her wings. An undistinguished entrepreneur can open up to new ideas if you justify their feasibility by addressing profitability and sustainability concerns.

Here are some ways that you can have a creative impact in an entrepreneurial firm:

- **Be innovative**
  Crafting ideas is not difficult if you have been in an industry for some time. If you are creative and analytical, you can not only showcase new ideas, but also justify putting the undistinguished entrepreneur's money into your ideas and demonstrate that the outcome you want will have a good return on investment. Write a business plan explaining the operating and marketing aspects of your idea, the risks, the expertise needed, who would be on the execution team, and the expected revenues. Adding prototypes and proofs-of-concept will bring your ideas to life and help the undistinguished entrepreneur visualize what you explain.
- **Give the undistinguished entrepreneur options and recommendations**
  A creative idea is sometimes difficult to be put into practice. If you present alternatives for achieving your plan, there is a good chance that the undistinguished entrepreneur will choose one of them.

However, do not feel insulted if the undistinguished entrepreneur reacts by finding fault with your work instead of praising your efforts and presentation. He or she may even question your knowledge of the industry in ways that express a lack of faith in your ability to accomplish what you propose.

Whether your ideas make the cut or not, it is important to remember that creativity always helps you in personal development. Also, creativity does not have to be artsy-creative or technology-creative; it may instead be vision-creative.[39] In his book *Value Migration*, Adrian Slywotzky talks about how, during the days of VAX computers, technology was the business-driver. With rapid imitation, global competition, and subsequent commoditization, margins shrunk for new technologies. Wal-Mart, Federal Express, and Southwest Airlines did not necessarily go after new technology—they experienced sustained value growth by understanding changing customer priorities and profit drivers in the industry. This vision and strategic understanding of their customers helped them to update their business designs and grow.

Starbucks also did it the same way by identifying what customers wanted. Bean procurement and roasting had been huge research focus areas at Starbucks—particularly the signature taste, aroma, and color. In addition to good coffee, however, Starbucks tried selling a unique experience, which was never offered to cafe customers before. The atmosphere that Starbucks created with the use of fine artwork, lights, and background music in its appealing store design (and by calling the servers *baristas*) helped Starbucks sell that experience through its coffee.[40] This experience was sold further to retail customers through Starbucks' partnerships with PepsiCo, Dreyer's Grand Ice Cream, and Kraft Foods among others, which helped Starbucks' growth and bonding with customers even further. Starbucks stores started selling food as well. Starbucks added another feather to its innovation cap when it started selling instant coffee. The innovation at Starbucks was not only in identifying the unmet need of "a unique Coffee experience" of its customers, which was leveraged in building a strong relationship, even outside the coffee shop, but also using that to survive tough economic times of the past few years.

Innovation does not have to be totally out of this world—it can come from existing practices and needs. So, having a good eye for what will make a difference, helps.

40

Improve the way decisions are taken and managed

NATASHA ANDERSON and her assistant Liz Abramsky won one battle after another in their endeavor to make Emerald Frozen Yogurt a success. During this process, they learned that the most important thing was to manage decision making in a way that there was no hurdle anywhere. Liz had a lot of industry knowledge and Natasha was the entrepreneur. Natasha wanted all the decisions in black and white, and Liz was always ready to go an extra mile to add color and reason to the final decisions. Natasha laid a huge emphasis on timeliness, in the belief that even the best decision if made too late can lose its value. Liz, on the other hand, believed a quick decision without supporting data would likely be meaningless. So, a balance between timeliness and good information was crucial.

Amitai Etzioni at George Washington University has shown that adaptive techniques can help with decision making. Etzioni explains the concept of mixed scanning,[41] which is a middle path between how decisions were taken between Natasha (*timely decisions*) and Liz (*decisions supported by a lot of data and facts*).

Back in Orange County, California, Dave Hansen had his own way of managing decisions at his IT firm. He had, for a long time, conducted meetings by standing in front of a roomful of people and almost making announcements (which he called meetings), and not looking for much response. Gradually, David brought more democracy into meetings and got everyone's opinion.

An entrepreneur's obsession with controlling events and ideas means that his or her style of taking decisions can be totally out of the common realm. The undistinguished entrepreneur likes the fact that important decisions are taken in meetings by an intellectual group with diverse ideas. However, at every meeting that is set up to elicit those ideas, the undistinguished entrepreneur states the core problem as he or she sees it and states what he or she will do to prevent it from occurring again. At the end of the meeting, the entrepreneur thanks everyone for contributing to create the illusion that the decision came out of an extensive discussion of employees' ideas. In such a setting, driving a move to professionally managed decisions require a lot of persuasion.

Try to determine whether the entrepreneur would be open to setting up a board of decision makers. A board would prevent one person's whims and fancies from determining what employees should be doing and how they should be doing it.

RMSI was founded in 1992, in a basement space in New Delhi by Ajay Lavakare, in a joint venture with Risk Management Software, Inc. (RMSI), CA, to serve the integrated Geographic Information Systems and software solutions space for natural hazard risk analysis and risk management. One of the first things Ajay Lavakare did to sustain the tremendous growth in the firm's early years was establish a board of decision makers and incorporate a solid decision-making structure in the organization. He instilled answerability and gave decision-making powers to the department heads and the team leads. The result: RMSI was ranked as the best employer across all industries in India for three years in a row, from 2006 to 2009, by *India's Best Companies to Work For* survey.[42]

The **SITA** formula can help you persuade the entrepreneur to improve the decision-making process.

- **Synergy**
  Start by agreeing with what the undistinguished entrepreneur says, without raising many arguments. Soon, he or she will agree with you. At that point, you can put forth your ideas and get them implemented.
- **Information**
  Before asking the undistinguished entrepreneur for an opinion or approval, think what information might be critical in making a decision, including facts and descriptions of similar situations. In other words, give the entrepreneur all the information necessary to get to a meaningful decision!

- **Timing**
  Choose the time to request a decision carefully. Present your data and recommendations only after getting a feel of the undistinguished entrepreneur's mood.
- **Attitude**
  Do not oppose the undistinguished entrepreneur just because you do not like institutional authority. It would perhaps be the worst mistake you could make, particularly if the entrepreneur is finally taking some steps toward good decisions and you are overruling his or her authority.

41

Support the hiring of professional senior management

GEORGE THOMPSON, the mechanical engineer in Michigan, started noticing a change—he was being taken more seriously by the entrepreneur. With this new-found confidence, George stepped up to bring more professionalism to the firm. His first request was to create a senior management team—to foster sound decision making by a group, as well as to protect individual employees from being dragged to the entrepreneur's guillotine every now and then.

For the selection process for the senior team member, George ensured that candidates are thoroughly validated against the rigorous demands of the undistinguished entrepreneur.

If you are conducting the interviews, make sure that the interviewees understand the current situation of the company and its goals and have the potential to align themselves with the firm. T.J. Rodgers of Cypress Semiconductor shared some basic rules of interviewing:[43]

- Get the executives (the entrepreneur in our case) to do the interviewing.
- Make interviews tough and technically demanding.
- Use interviews to assess strengths and weaknesses.
- Assess cultural fit.

Here are some interviewees you would be wise to avoid:

- An overly ambitious person (unless you want to handle a difficult person in addition to the entrepreneur you are handling now).
- A show-off. Every office has an employee who never gets tired of repeated pronouncements regarding his or her achievements. These recruits are unproductive and very soon alienate their team members.
- A bully. Bullies put pressure on other workers and managers to abandon good strategies and ideas.
- A potential "eternal honeymooner." Every employee enjoys a honeymoon period. For the vast majority, it is short. During the honeymoon period, the employee is treated reasonably well. The eternal honeymooner does not seem to understand that the honeymoon will eventually end. If you hire such a person, watch how the person takes to the new position and how soon he or she finds ways to meet the undistinguished entrepreneur's perpetual demands.
- Revenue drivers. The revenue drivers don't know the business but promise to bring in lots of money. If the promise isn't realized, the negative effect may rub off on you. After all, who recruited this employee?
- Employee well-being advocate. This interviewee talks a lot about leading a well-rounded life and the great

importance of everyone's visiting parks and taking yoga classes as a group. He or she suffers less stress than do other employees. However, most undistinguished entrepreneurs are more concerned about sales, outcomes, and increasing productivity. Reconciling these two opposing sets of agenda becomes your responsibility.

42

Mentor your subordinates, particularly the difficult ones

JUAN LOPEZ, from the engineering consulting firm, wanted to define and realize a vision for the company. He started by trying to align employee goals with those of the firm. He encouraged a lot of interaction among employees and started a mentoring program to coach the new hires. If his Storming–Norming plan ever hit a hurdle, Juan knew how to manage team issues and boldly maneuvered his program through all such resistances.

Sustained success at an entrepreneurial firm depends on how people within the company interact. Mentoring your subordinates should certainly be one of your strategic goals. It does not involve a lot of work—you can start by telling them a few things about entrepreneurial business. You can help them in setting and achieving milestones and subsequently, find a way to reward them for achievement.

However, your subordinates will not always get along with you or follow your directions. For those subordinates, you may want to try the following strategies:

- Give guidance but do not do the subordinate's work. If you are continually solving your subordinate's problems, that person is not working for you—you are working for him or her.

- Research the subordinate's performance and records. A thorough evaluation puts you in a good position to deal with a difficult subordinate.
- Initiate an in-person meeting with the subordinate to discuss problems in a non-confrontational way.
- Approach issues in a logical, rational way—focus on what is right, not on what you want.
- Never show resentment toward a subordinate, particularly in a group setting. The goal is to solve the problem, not to injure the subordinate.
- Check the alignment of the subordinate's goals with those of the firm's goals.
- Act as a coach and share knowledge with the subordinate.

These strategies will help you establish a habit of rational thought in the firm and also get you a friendly base of subordinates who will listen to you and help you in times of need.

43

Apprise the entrepreneur of your career goals, without asking for a raise or reward

WHEN Paula Silva joined an entrepreneur-owned financial services firm in suburban Rio de Janeiro, Brazil, she had no experience at commodities trading. She had come straight out of school, with a specialization in finance. The entrepreneur was aggressive and successful in a cutthroat market and had lost only a few bets in his whole career in commodities. The culture of the firm was very similar to the entrepreneur's own personality. He had worked with some of the larger investment banks and trading firms in the country before starting his own. During Paula's orientation, he had smiled and said: "Why make money for others when I have a business model here that I could use?"

Paula and others in the firm never volunteered a conversation with the entrepreneur as they feared (and somewhat wanted to stay away from) his commander-type personality traits. However, after a year of no advancement, Paula began to suspect that her skills and performance were being underrated. One afternoon, Paula finally got a chance to talk to the entrepreneur while they were working on a presentation together. As Paula was putting together the slides, she mentioned the projects that she was working on and how she felt they could have been better handled. The entrepreneur took interest in her perspectives, and in a couple of months, Paula was working with some key clients and had gotten herself a salary raise.

Far too many of us are afraid to demand what we are worth, thankful just to have a job and fearful of being fired. Many of us hope and expect at the outset that the undistinguished entrepreneur will turn out to be a great mentor, provide us with a path to success, and always keep our career progression in mind. Some of us are fortunate enough to find an entrepreneur who thinks that way but for the vast majority of us, the undistinguished entrepreneur plots only his or her own path and, perhaps, an early retirement.

Chances are that the undistinguished entrepreneur does not have a clue to your dreams. Just as you need to manage the entrepreneur's tasks, you need to keep him or her aware of your tasks and the career track you want. It will help to clarify your expectations and, in response, encourage the entrepreneur to make the firm a better place for you. If you do not express your goals, he or she will always be under the impression that you are satisfied with what you have.

No matter how incompetent or inexperienced the entrepreneur appears, he or she probably has solid experience in at least one area. The entrepreneur may also be quite knowledgeable about what is needed to progress along a career path within the industry.

We have already looked at the importance of training for both individuals and groups within the company; it is essential to enable companies to retain talent and grow amid competition. So, go to conferences, seminars, and build friendships in the industry. Enroll in training and workshops and keep certifications and skills up-to-date. Use networking opportunities to the fullest; the more options you have, the less pressure at work you will experience.

Whether or not the undistinguished entrepreneur has been tracking your growth, it's your responsibility to keep him or her informed about your successes. You can also remind the entrepreneur of your credentials (and accomplishments) and mention thoughtfully how your colleagues in other firms are growing in their responsibilities and titles; this might trigger a discussion on giving you a raise as well.

Now, this is where all the negotiation skills you have learned all your life come into play. What used to be salary negotiation meetings are now 360-degree employee reviews. No matter which form the negotiations take, you need to keep the entrepreneur apprised of your goals and your interest in growth within the firm.

44

Update the firm's practices

PATRICK KYOSHI's father ran a London-based pharmaceutical company and wanted Patrick to join the family business. However, Patrick chose to attend a school of hospitality management instead. After brief stints with some of the leading theme parks, hotels, and luxury travel groups in the United Kingdom, he decided to look for a job in France.

Rich Durand, the Paris travel agency entrepreneur who believed strongly in luck, had been noticing a rapid downtrend in travel bookings. That is when he came across Patrick's resume. Patrick had traveled extensively and been exposed to best practices at several travel and hospitality firms; he understood that building culture as well as instituting improved practices could help the growth of a firm.

Rich hired Patrick, and together they started packaging flights and hotel stays into more affordable bundles. Then they looked at strategic alliances with vacation home and timeshare organizations, entertainment ticket discounters, and other travel and tourism organizations. In six months, with limited resources and without any bait-and-switch offerings, they had diversified, established several partnerships, and kept the revenues flowing.

In a changing economy, the companies that survive are those who stay ahead of the rest by improving their processes, implementing customer-centric solutions, and keeping their employees happy.

Adrian Slywotzky identified three important phases in business design—value inflow, stability, and value outflow.[44] If the business is in the value inflow phase, the entrepreneur should capture as much revenue as possible. If the business is experiencing the stability phase, the entrepreneur should work both to sustain the business and identify new dimensions and practices that could bring more value. If you are noticing a value outflow, propose to the entrepreneur a change in the current business design and move closer to current customer preferences by changing practices along with a new business design.

However, not everyone in the firm might be as eager as you are to learn best practices and preach their adoption. They would rather wait and see whether or not the undistinguished entrepreneur wants changes in the current practices.

Here are some suggestions for promoting the adoption of best practices to everyone.

- Suggest practices that contribute to the undistinguished entrepreneur's goals.
- Demonstrate to everyone in the firm how a new practice can bring positive results and how the change from current practice can be managed effectively.
- Use visuals in your presentation and avoid being too wordy. Check out blog sites such as Garr Reynolds' www.presentationzen.com,[45] among others where you can get a lot of ideas on designing simple yet impactful messages.
- Point out similar successful implementations elsewhere.

The undistinguished entrepreneur has to review the suggested new practices and ensure availability of resources for their implementation.

Tying new practice adoption to an employee-rewards program is another good way to get the new practice ball rolling. Increased employee motivation through employee rewards will help new practices to be adopted faster and will also allow the entrepreneur to resolve any possible employee dissatisfaction.

45

Be an asset, not a liability

JEFFREY PFEFFER at Stanford Graduate School of Business has explained the importance of the workforce and how companies such as Southwest Airlines and Nordstrom have succeeded because of their very productive and highly motivated employees.[46] This competitive advantage is not that easy to imitate as it involves comprehensive culture building within the firm.

Graham Taylor had great ideas—and several vices. He did not go to college, and started working at a young age, mostly for the steady cash flow for merrymaking and revelry. As he grew older, he got more exposure to people in his industry and built strong connections there. He spent long hours wining and dining his business friends and clients. Building relationships quickly became his strength.

When Graham joined a publishing firm in New York, he advanced faster than everyone else as he was friendly and quickly acquired industry knowledge. However, he used his position to provide himself with posh vacations that he got used to expensing as client meetings—until he was caught by the entrepreneur. He had a job but was no longer considered a valuable asset. Graham changed his ways but he could never win back the trust he had abused.

If you are an expense-account abuser, you are certainly not an asset. Once you have been typecast as that, it can become very difficult to get business trips or meals approved even if the business need is genuine. The undistinguished entrepreneur sees your uncalled-for spending and writes you off as someone who cannot pass a client dining event with the corporate credit card in your wallet. You gradually move away from being taken seriously as an asset by the entrepreneur.

Do you think *you* are considered an asset to your firm? Employees do show up on the balance sheet, literally as well as figuratively. There is a line on the assets side of the sheet where the talent of the workforce is measured together with other qualitative factors; these are called intangible assets. Although not specific, this item on the balance sheet definitely includes the asset value of company workers in some way.

Being an asset to the entrepreneur has a much wider meaning than just increasing the sales revenues. As an asset, you contribute to the firm's goals, strategic partnerships, culture, new products, and new practices. Cutting spending, particularly on expensive trade shows or unnecessary product advertising, also increases your asset value.

If you demonstrate success with a few low-cost ideas, you will be seen by the undistinguished entrepreneur as highly productive and highly motivated and will find your other ideas accepted as well. Returns on investment often take a long time to come and when they do, they often come in small numbers. As a result, it is easier to succeed on a small project with a relatively lower budget over a shorter term, thus giving a better ROI picture to the entrepreneur. Remember: One smart idea and you get it all.

The key to becoming an asset is to do something extra that is not expected of you. Take up additional opportunities and new initiatives, offer suggestions on how the entrepreneur can

improve production, observe the interaction of coworkers, and strive to find ways to promote harmony at work.

If you work to make the entrepreneur realize how much your efforts have contributed to the firm, your employee value (EV) will soar and the extra mile you walked will be heartily rewarded.

46

Make yourself indispensable

ONE thing that Juan Lopez, Rajiv Sinha, Linh Chun, Liz Abramsky, and Patrick Kyoshi had in common was that over time, each became indispensable at their entrepreneurial firms. They had different skills, backgrounds, interests, and characteristics, yet they entered circles of trust and became agents of change and growth.

Indispensable employees are well-liked. They make the undistinguished entrepreneur's job easier and they earn the respect of colleagues. Indispensable employees also tend to survive a layoff. Good attitude, high degree of flexibility, willingness to work hard, and adherence to the entrepreneur's standards—all go a long way toward securing your position.

Even if you feel you are indispensable by virtue of your hard work or special skills, it is a good idea to consider making yourself indispensable in other ways.

- **Take initiative and ownership**
  Do not stop at doing what is assigned to you. Exceed expectations.
- **Fix problems and deliver trust**
  If you are wrong, own up to your mistake and work to fix it. Be willing to help solve others' problems as well

as your own. Deliver high quality every time and make yourself the most valuable player (MVP).

- **Examine your goals and be dependable**
  Ask yourself how your goals can be aligned with the firm's goals. Also, if you are strategically aligned, are you dependable?
- **Empathize**
  Show that you care about the success of others and demonstrate a good work ethic, humility, and commitment.
- **Look good**
  Strive for good health, fitness, and appearance (you do not need to live inside the Gucci outlet or sleep at the gym).
- **Adapt**
  Keep tabs on the changes in your industry, your company, and the requirements of your own position. Re-educate, retrain, and adapt yourself accordingly.

Entrepreneurs often think that they can get by without anybody else's help (as they have that do-it-all characteristic). So, it is important to make the undistinguished entrepreneur realize the importance of employees. Educate the entrepreneur that the departure of a capable employee—who has been treated badly—is never a good idea, as any new hire takes a long time to get to speed, thus incurring opportunity costs and loss of institutional knowledge to the entrepreneurial firm. Disgruntled employees' leaving can be even costlier if they have patents or knowledge that competing firms can leverage.

47

Remind the entrepreneur to think twice before purchasing or hiring services

DO you remember Graham Taylor at the New York publishing firm? His problem was lavishness and reckless spending—with company resources. Imagine if it is the entrepreneur instead who is wasteful. That is an even more serious problem!

Rich Durand, the travel agency entrepreneur in Paris, went through a phase of extravagant spending. He hired employees without thoroughly interviewing them and spent quite a bit of the firm's money on personal travel, which was his passion and perhaps the reason that he had chosen the travel industry. When Patrick Kyoshi joined the agency, he brought Rich under control. Rich started using what he already had and stopped overspending.

The undistinguished entrepreneur does not even bother to hide unnecessary or personal expenditures in the belief that his (or her) personal purchases are in some way connected to the company he (or she) started. The problem is not the spending itself, but the indifference toward the value of the product to the company.

If the undistinguished entrepreneur likes someone and decides to create a new position, ask the entrepreneur where he or she sees a need to add staff. If the entrepreneur needs a new car (for the office) because the present one is not good enough, ask him how that will solve the existing issues at hand.

The undistinguished entrepreneur also tends to outsource minor obligations and is not careful of expenditures such as staff vacation and holiday allowances and other administrative details. Remind the entrepreneur of ways the saved money could be put to better use.

To curb the undistinguished entrepreneur's spending, you can bring some fiscal discipline into purchasing decisions. Here are some suggestions for introducing fiscal controls:

- Recommend that research and training on core competencies be done in-house rather than contracted out.
- Research the firm's needs before the entrepreneur spends money. For example, ask why an IT analyst is needed when there are not enough IT projects to justify one.

- Make a list of items and services to be purchased and prioritize them according to the need.
- In any budget, include deadlines for purchase decisions.
- Encourage delays for all impulsive purchases.

An expenditure-tracking system and an approval process can help to curb spending. Ask the entrepreneur to start giving up a few things, such as holding office parties for unimportant occasions or traveling to attend routine conferences in distant countries.

You should also encourage the entrepreneur to stop comparing his or her operations with those of other leading firms, including competitors (firms in the same business space) that he or she feels somehow "akin" to. Aping other companies for hiring resources or buying equipment may lead to draining useful company resources.

We all seek commonality (subconsciously) with one another and get influenced to do certain common things—even if there are not many relevant attributes that are affably common. So does the undistinguished entrepreneur. A research team under Noah Goldstein at UCLA's Anderson School of Management examined the persuasive power of hotel pamphlets that asked hotel guests to reuse towels (in an effort to conserve water).[47] The team changed the wording in the conventional pamphlets to see if different wording would bring about changes in behavior. The team observed that with one group that was told about former guests in the *same room* having reused towels, there was a 33 percent jump in reuse even though the message was largely the same. Somehow, customers seemed to feel a commonality or affinity with the guests who had stayed in that room. Such a bond due to commonality with fellow entrepreneurs in the same industry attracts the entrepreneur as well, but does not do anything to further business.

The entrepreneur should instead assess customers' changing priorities and adapt to their needs, looking more carefully at products that would yield more profit and getting rid of those that are dragging the company down with high overheads. In addition, the entrepreneur should keep operations running lean and hold on to as much cash as possible.

48

Keep the entrepreneur's blue-eyed boy on your team

IT's worthwhile to try to keep all employees on your side, but it is particularly important to keep the entrepreneur's favorite employees there.

When Rajiv Sinha started with the entrepreneur, he ran into some resistance from the much-trusted vice president. The vice president had started at the bottom and risen through the ranks after years of hard work. He could not imagine how a young, foreign-educated, MBA could tell him how to improve the organization. When he heard Rajiv's first suggestion, he laughed and asked: "Why don't you work here for a year and see for yourself?"

Rajiv listened and learned everything from the vice president that a mentee could. At the end of his first year, he paid a visit to the vice president and his wife and gave the wife a beautiful gift to thank her husband for making his learning so easy and valuable. A month later when the entrepreneur was high on a whim cycle and came down on Rajiv for not being more "serious" about his prospective accounts, it was the vice president who came forth to save Rajiv.

Linh Chun had a similar experience. When she started working on a gap report, one of the entrepreneur's advisors was disapproving, calling the effort "a waste of time." However, when she implemented the plan and the outcomes came as she predicted, the entire board of advisors was pleased, and particularly the one who had doubted her at the beginning.

The undistinguished entrepreneur will always favor certain employees and include them within a circle of trust regardless of what they do. They may have been admitted to the circle for their looks or sense of style, communication skills, achievements, or some creative idea that worked (or one that supported the entrepreneur's flights of fancy).

When *favorite* employees (or *blue-eyed* boys) do something that betrays the entrepreneur's trust, they generally regain it very quickly. I know of one incident in which a favorite manager punched a client at a workshop; the entrepreneur treated the event as an amusing incident. A favorite employee has a critical advantage: he or she is like the entrepreneur in some way. Take an unbiased and objective look at the entrepreneur and the favorite and ask yourself what they have in common or what bonds them.

Establish a feeling of camaraderie with the favorite(s), and with everyone around you who matters to you, in your position. This is again where you have to look at the importance of assessing the codependence of your relationships and how you can help others to grow with you, if they are appreciated and treated well.

The downfall of the blue-eyed person often comes when he (or she) sets expectations too high. Eventually, not meeting those expectations becomes a point for his or her dismissal. So, be sure to document everything you do at work. No matter how many favorites come and go, or what happens in the future, your record will always reflect how important you are to the firm.

49

Bring realism into forecasting

ACCORDING to George Bernard Shaw: "*We are made wise not by the recollection of our past, but by the responsibility for our future.*"

However, for Natasha Anderson, past experience was very important in creating the Emerald Frozen Yogurt brand and also in providing statistical data for running forecasts. Liz Abramsky, on the other hand, knew that people's tastes change so fast that Emerald Frozen Yogurt would have to respond to the latest trends or be wiped out.

Liz believed that the frozen yogurt market was a fad (short product life cycle) and though monetizing it was easy, forecasting was difficult. She had studied the frozen-dessert market (ice cream, yogurt, sherbet, and tofu-based products, among others) closely and had noticed how total consumption grew minimally but shifted frequently from one product to the other. That is when she recommended adding Japanese and Italian ice creams and even some baked novelties to the product line to attract a diverse group of customers. Natasha bought the idea, and the results were fabulous.

For Paula Silva, along with her new position at the Brazilian asset management firm came significant responsibility. One such responsibility was forecasting sales. Paula surveyed several families and their willingness to take risks and studied the results. Paula then divided her target clients into psychographic segments; for each segment, she prescribed risk tolerances and a mix of financial investments. To promote these packages, she also considered factors such as increasing competition, decreasing margins, and price sensitivity within the different segments. She ran a pilot test on a small, representative market and extrapolated the outcome for forecasting the larger market. After a year, when the entrepreneur compared Paula's forecasts to the actual outcomes, he found that they were very close to reality.

Forecasting the entrepreneurial firm's profit a year in advance is difficult. However, it is normal for the undistinguished entrepreneur to miss red flags and be overly optimistic about the future.

When thinking about forecasting savings, research has shown that the threat of loss is felt more intensely than the possibility of gain. Thus, when you show the undistinguished entrepreneur that the company can save $1,000 by taking a given action, you may not be taken seriously. However, if you tell the entrepreneur that if you do *not* take that action the company will incur a $1,000 loss, you will get immediate attention.

In recent years, business forecasting has evolved into a scientific and statistical modeling effort with a variety of algorithms. Business forecasting involves a wide range of tools, from spreadsheets prepared with MS Excel to powerful enterprise resource planning and customer relationship management tools. Many other technologies can be applied to produce cost, revenue, risk, and opportunity projections with a high degree of accuracy.

Larger corporations use forecasting models that are based on time series historical data and established formulae as they have had stable sales patterns over the past several years. For the undistinguished entrepreneur, however, forecasting has often been based on gut feeling rather than real data. The undistinguished entrepreneur produces a forecast without much historical information and with data from only a few customers. With so many unknowns, the entrepreneur's forecasting depends on just the number of orders he or she received last month or the number of new customers that have made purchases in the same period the previous year.

Focusing on services and products that generate sustainable and recurring revenues yield better forecasts. In addition, useful ideas from employees, brand-building, and potential growth through diversification can be of immense help to the undistinguished entrepreneur. Studying case histories of how similar firms in similar situations undertook expansion—geographic, functional or industrial—also helps.

Adrian Slywotzky has revealed another dimension of forecasting.[48] Changing customer preferences widen the competitive playing field and existing businesses may find themselves fighting new competitors from unconventional markets and other industries for the same customers.

"We take the labor out of your delivery," is what the Los Angeles company—Ellie & Melissa, the Baby Planners—promised.[49] Their plan was similar to wedding planners except that here they would help expectant mothers plan their parenthood, such as giving tips on things to buy, where all to go, and who to contact. The entrepreneurs forecast that they could easily handle marketing and did not foresee the changing price sensitivity due to the down economy as a problem. With the economy, household budgets and preferences changed as well. Subsequently, the entrepreneurs Ellie Miller and Melissa Gould had to re-strategize the business and retool their plan—they still offer consulting services—however, their main focus now is advising baby product manufacturers on what customers (expectant parents) want. And they have seen enormous success with this new business model.

Closely related to identifying changing customer preferences is the ability of the firm to recognize industry changes. Guy Kawasaki of Garage Technology Ventures brought out the importance of jumping a curve and not waiting so long to make a move that the curve goes extinct. He cited the example of firms that farmed and sold ice and how they could not conceive the widespread use of refrigerators and missed a great opportunity.

Thus, forecasting should not only take into account the trends from previous years and loyal accounts, but also consider changing customer preferences, changing compliance issues, changing competitor prices, new go-to-market mechanisms, and changing technology.

50

Help the entrepreneur to connect with the firm's clients

AFTER jumping through numerous hoops, George Thompson finally entered the entrepreneur's inner circle of trust and suggested him to establish a stronger connection with clients and to learn from them.

Similarly, Juan Lopez urged the entrepreneur to get closer to the customers and participate in knowledge sharing by writing papers with them, conducting web conferences, and introducing them to other customers.

Jack Dangermond, one of the several pioneers who studied at the Harvard Laboratory for Computer Graphics and Spatial Analysis, founded the Environmental Systems Research Institute (ESRI) in 1969 with a vision that computer mapping and analysis could help us design a better future. Under Dangermond's leadership, that vision has continued to guide ESRI and his clients in creating enterprise-wide systems and advanced technologies to make a difference. Dangermond has resorted to connections not only as a visionary, but also as a trusted advisor on Geographic Information Systems (GIS). White papers, customer case studies, blogs, strong partnership network, and other vehicles have helped ESRI evolve from a small research group to an organization recognized as the world leader in GIS software development.

With social networks on the rise, the entrepreneur has both the means and the need to connect. Connection makes selling easier. When the entrepreneur connects with a prospect, he or she does so as a friend, a trusted colleague or advisor.

Guy Kawasaki showed in his book *The Art of the Start* how entrepreneurs' recruitment of evangelists among their customers could help them in building their businesses.[50] The simplest way is to ask the customers to become evangelists and empower them with the tools to do so. When customers and prospects talk to each other, the effect is to build the brand as well as increase sales. The biggest deals are often sealed without interviews or responding to tenders—they are done through relationships.

In order to be closer to customers, encourage the entrepreneur to take some of the following steps:

- Writing white papers that address customers' needs and show how the firm can tailor its services to serve them.
- Seeking customers' opinions. Customers will feel more attached to the firm and its products if their inputs are considered. If their ideas can be incorporated into a product (such as a software application), they will feel a natural ownership in the product.
- Writing case studies and building brand awareness in different market segments.
- Making the marketing attractive at the grassroots (or the end user) level. Use webinars, newsletters, blogs, feeds, discussion forums, and user group meetings to create and maintain connections to customers.
- Conducting experience-sharing events that bring prospects and existing customers together to talk to each other.

Connecting with customers can provide other critical information about the market, competitors, and products, as well as provide valuable information regarding any issues they have with company's employees or services.

51

Consider quitting only as a last resort

GEORGE BERNARD SHAW said, "*Life isn't about finding yourself. Life is about creating yourself.*"

If the undistinguished entrepreneur does not improve in spite of your best efforts and seems to be heading for a crash, it might be a good time for you to consider changing jobs. You do not want to go down with a sinking ship.

Remember that through adversity comes greatness. If you feel that you are facing extraordinarily harsh conditions in your job, you are destined to do something great and turn some other firm around, if not this one.

Put a short resignation letter together. In the letter, be sure to thank the entrepreneur for giving you the opportunity to be a part of the firm (why burn bridges?). Mention the last working day there. It is a good idea not to write anything bad about the firm.

You can also ask for a letter of recommendation from the undistinguished entrepreneur. Find out about the benefits you would receive, such as continuing health insurance, pay for unused vacation and sick time, and the right to hold on to your retirement savings.

Strategic Lessons

THE undistinguished entrepreneur may have hit a few home runs in the past, and ever since then, spent his or her energies trying to cash in on the existing model. The undistinguished entrepreneur should look for ways to reinforce and build on victories and hedge risks. In this section, we have looked into strategies that can not only sustain the firm but advance it into new dimensions.

Most strategy consulting firms review a firm's existing situation, help the firm to identify goals, and provide an assessment of the gaps between where the firm wants to be and where it is. The assessment helps the firm refine goals and follow a roadmap to greatness. Your strategic effort for the entrepreneur should mirror this effort but take it a step further to see that the plans actually work.

In the Strategic section, we have looked at a few major areas of strategy development:

- Organizational strategies (focusing on profitability, instilling more clarity in workflows, improving decision-making flows, updating practices, bringing increased realism into forecasting, preaching caution in purchasing or hiring services).
- Strategic planning (understanding long-term goals, recognizing and supporting innovation, hiring professional senior management).
- Strategies to help identify roles for firm growth (stating your career goals, being an asset rather than a liability,

mentoring your subordinates, supporting the entrepreneur's connections with clients, making oneself indispensable).

Once you have defined good strategies, the cycle of improvement (*kaizen*) will continue. Check your procedures again. Are they in tune with best practices? Check the behaviors again. Does the firm's culture need to be changed? Finally, come back to your strategies. Are there new strategies that could bring more harmony to the firm, grow it more organically, and sustain its success?

■

Strategic Clinic

LET us help a couple of entrepreneurs with strategies that will work for their firms.

Entrepreneur 5: The beauty salon and spa

Our entrepreneur worked at a leading cosmetic company before she went independent and bought a salon. She added some spa services and had great sales the first year, but costs were high. She raised the prices and, contrary to her fears, the traffic increased further. Business had never been so good. She got carried away by that victory.

Other spas had begun to offer sophisticated spa services such as microdermabrasion and laser hair removal but the entrepreneur did not update her services. She was facing competition from services that had traditionally been offered by medical offices. She realized the effects of this when she lost some regular clients to competitors and noticed that employee turnover was slowly increasing. She had no employee training program, nor did she encourage teamwork at the salon. As a result, knowledge transfer was difficult and each employee who left represented a significant loss of expertise.

Now, the entrepreneur is thinking of selling the business. What is your advice?

Entrepreneur 6: Furniture sales and refinishing

The entrepreneur owns a furniture manufacturing company and wants to diversify due to the uncertain prospects of the furniture industry. He has decided to move into furniture assembly and repair services as well as prefabricated homes market.

The entrepreneur's due diligence revealed the following facts:

- Competitors and substitutes are geography specific
- Fixed costs are high and margins are low due to competition
- Brand equity does not play a major role
- The industry faces cyclical demands
- The market is growing but consumers are becoming more and more cost sensitive

Based on the due diligence, the entrepreneur divided his marketing dollars among different lines. He used the following percentage allocations:

- Original furniture business: 40 percent
- Furniture installation and repair services: 30 percent
- Prefabricated homes: 30 percent

Review the allocations. How would you have allocated the budget if you were the budgeting chief at this firm?

■

Notes and References

Preface

1. Entrepreneurs drive technology

Vinod Khosla's greatest passion is being a mentor to entrepreneurs. In 1986, Vinod joined Kleiner Perkins, where he continues to be an affiliated partner. In 2004, Vinod formed Khoslaventures, funded entirely with family funds. Vinod currently serves on the boards of a few companies and is also a founding board member of the Indian School of Business. He is also a supporter of many microfinance organizations in India and Africa.

2. Hiring of graduates by large companies near its lowest historic levels in 2010

Hibah Yousuf, CNNMoney.com. "Job Outlook for 2010 Grads: Still Stinks." Article available at http://money.cnn.

com/2009/11/17/news/economy/college_graduates_jobs/index.htm (accessed January 2010).

The Study by Michigan State University's Collegiate Employment Research Institute has identified that the small establishments (less than eight employees), fast-growth companies (9–100 employees), and small companies (101–500 employees) will increase hiring, while medium-size companies (500–3,999 employees) and large companies (greater than 4,000 employees) will decrease their annual recruitment in 2010.

Acknowledgments

3. Bill Cockrum a top entrepreneurship professor in the US

See article Judi Crowe and Lourdes Hernandez, "The Best Entrepreneurship Teachers." Article available at http://www.businessweek.com/1996/51/b350644.htm (accessed on July 29, 2011).

I. Procedural Ways: Prologue

4. Small businesses experience similar problems

Neil C. Churchill and Virginia Lewis, "The Five Stages of Small Business Growth," *Harvard Business Review* No. 83301 (May–June 1983): 1–8.

The article discusses a framework for small businesses in different developmental stages.

Chapter 1

5. Coercive, pacesetting leaders negatively impact the work climate

Daniel Goleman, "Leadership That Gets Results," *Harvard Business Review* No. R00204 (March–April 2000): 81–82.

Daniel Goleman is an internationally known psychologist who lectures frequently to professional groups, business audiences, and on college campuses. Goleman showed in his research six different styles of leadership (coercive, authoritative, affiliative, democratic, pacesetting, and coaching) which affected the organizational climate and hence performance in different ways.

Chapter 7

6. Using a simple goal-based system

T.J. Rodgers, "No Excuses Management," *Harvard Business Review* No. 90409 (July–August 1990): 5–7.

T.J. Rodgers has shared his experiences in this article and explained how simple tools can help keeping track of goals.

7. Managing team resources

The Project Management Institute (Newtown Square, Pennsylvania) (www.pmi.org) is the world's leading not-for-profit membership association for the project management profession.

Chapter 9

8. Gifts should only be given when relationships are strong

I spoke with Noah Goldstein of UCLA's Anderson School of Management, the author of *Yes!: 50 Scientifically Proven Ways to Be Persuasive* (Free Press, 2008) at the 2010 UCLA Alumni Day. His presentation also featured other persuasion studies—why gifts should be significant, customized, and unexpected; asymmetric perception between the favor-doer and the favor-receiver; how some car-wash companies retain customers by punching extra clicks on their punch cards to encourage them to continue and get the free wash; people with memory decay need reminders; state the negatives and then the positives; and how hotel guests find commonality with guests who had stayed in the same room earlier.

Chapter 11

9. Allocating a weekly budget to every manager

T.J. Rodgers, op. cit.

Chapter 13

10. State the negatives and then the positives

Noah Goldstein, op. cit.

11. Demonstrate to the entrepreneur that you have made progress

Joseph C. Nunes and Xavier Drèze, "The Endowed Progress Effect: How Artificial Advancement Increases Effort," *Journal of Consumer Research* 32 (2006): 504–12.

Chapter 14

12. Asymmetric perception

Noah Goldstein, op. cit.

13. Memory decay

Noah Goldstein, op. cit.

Chapter 16

14. Goal System replaced bureaucratic obscurity

T.J. Rodgers, op. cit.

Chapter 17

15. Delhi Technological University

P.B. Sharma, the Vice Chancellor of the Delhi Technological University, has not only laid emphasis on the need of green enterprises, but also pointed out the lack of ideation, technology incubation, and product development in colleges. In a recent convention, Sharma spoke of the need of getting academia close to the industry to better address the societal needs in India, and also the need of knowledge enterprise hubs for the promotion of Technopreneurship.

16. Indian School of Business

After being repeatedly ranked as one of the top 20 business schools by *The Financial Times*, ISB's Ajit Rangnekar decided to revamp the school's mission, making it more about fostering equitable socioeconomic growth in the country and serving the emerging economy.

17. Companies who make training a high priority can gain competitive advantage

Jeffrey Pfeffer, *Competitive Advantage through People* (Boston: Harvard Business School Press, 1994). Jeffrey Pfeffer shows how the source of competitive advantage shifts over time. Sustainable competitive advantage comes due to factors that: (*a*) are difficult to imitate, (*b*) provide positive benefits, and (*c*) distinguish from other competitors. In his examples, he shows how management of people has become an important competitive advantage factor, besides technology, patents, and other strategic reasons.

Chapter 18

18. Making a firm financially sound

Herbert Woodward, "Management Strategies for Small Companies," *Harvard Business Review* No. 76111 (January 1976): 113–21.

In his article, Woodward talks about underlying weaknesses in numerous small businesses that can adversely affect the return on investment. Some of these problems arise when the business expands beyond what a manager can handle.

19. Importance of cash in keeping any business competitive

John O. Whitney, "Turnaround Management Every Day," *Harvard Business Review* No. 87514 (September–October 1987): 49–55.

An excellent article where Whitney focuses on the need of turnarounds in bringing failing companies back to life. He discusses ways to better understand and use the company's finances and redefine the organizational structure to bring more efficiency in operations.

Procedural Lessons

20. Jeff Wilke

I spoke with Jeff Wilke when he visited Anderson School, UCLA, in 2002 and got a chance to understand some of the operational techniques that Amazon had used to improve its efficiency.

II. Behavioral Ways: Prologue

21. Richard Giorla

Owner of the famous Cardio Barre fitness in Studio City and the author of the book *Raise the Barre* (New York: William

Morrow, 2006) tracks every detail of transactions. Please visit the company website at www.cardiobarre.com to learn about Richard Giorla and his company.

Chapter 21

22. What you should avoid at all cost is being typecast

Nobel laureate Daniel Kahneman and Amos Tversky have shown that during decision making, individuals tend to excessively rely on specific information (anchor) and then adjust to that for other elements. As a result, with the anchor set, there is a bias toward that.

Chapter 22

23. ADD Entrepreneurs Research Project

See the website http://www.kmarshack.com/ADD-and-ADHD/ADD-Entrepreneurs-Research-Project.html (accessed in April 2010).

Dr Kathy J. Marshack's institute is conducting a study to learn more about the challenges the ADD entrepreneur faces creating focus and balance in his or her life and correct any problem that the ADD entrepreneur faces. According to her, the results will aid in harnessing the ADD entrepreneur's creativity, salvaging the ADD entrepreneur's self-esteem, and restoring healthy family life. The bottom line is to add more solid businesses to the American economy.

Chapter 24

24. Drucker's philosophy

Rick Wartzman, "Manage your Boss." Article available at http://www.druckerinstitute.com/showpage.aspx?Section=RP&PageID=113 (accessed in April 2010).

Rick Wartzman, the executive director of the Drucker Institute at Claremont Graduate University, discusses Peter Drucker's teaching, which emphasizes that your success depends not just on how well you do your job, but also depends on how well your manager does his or hers. Rick was very kind to give his inputs and comments on this book's text as well.

Chapter 25

25. FedEx's Fred Smith

David Lewin (Anderson, UCLA), Debra Dalle (Anderson, UCLA), and Mr Charles W. Thomson (FedEx), "Federal Express Inc.," *Anderson School of Management Case* (March 1992): 1–6.

The case shows how FedEx introduced its service in the vastly untapped overnight delivery market. There was a compressed version that was used at the Anderson School in 2008 and 2009 for the first and second Global Business Leadership Competition that featured MBA students' teams from around the world, competing for prizes.

26. An entrepreneur crafts strategy perpetually

Henry Mintzberg, "Crafting Strategy," *Harvard Business Review* 65, no. 4 (July–August 1987): 66–74.

Henry Mintzberg and a research team at McGill tracked strategies of 11 organizations, over several decades of their history. The team developed list of important actions that these organizations took and labeled them as strategies after identifying patterns in these actions. Then the team represented graphically all these strategies to identify periods of their development and used interviews and reports to study key points of change in the strategic history of each firm to develop conclusions about the process of strategy formation.

Chapter 27

27. High degree of uniqueness and high value to customers

I attended a lecture by Guy Kawasaki at UCLA. There, he talked about how an entrepreneur should "get going" and never spend too much time perfecting a product. Instead, he or she should take the product to market and create successive versions to get a better product. He also talked about jumping the curve and not missing windows of opportunity—he cited how ice makers who made ice at manufacturing plants and put the 19th century ice harvesters out of business missed out on refrigerators as they never challenged the known and embraced the unknown.

28. Takes quite a few different qualities and practices to be creative

Silvano Arieti, *Creativity: The Magic Synthesis* (New York: Basic Books, 1976).

Arieti's book outlined an elaborate theory for understanding what goes on in the act of creativity.

29. Creativity and strategy are driven by corporate capabilities gained

Henry Mintzberg, op. cit.

Chapter 28

30. Wholly rational decisions are extremely difficult

Amitai Etzioni, "Humble Decision Making," *Harvard Business Review* No. 89406 (July–August 1989): 122–26.

With too much data and too little time, executives must often take decisions with only partial information. This article discusses how data overload can be dealt effectively with adaptive decision making or mixed scanning by considering a broad range of facts and choices followed by a detailed examination of only a subset (and not all) of those choices.

31. Even the toughest change can be made significantly easier

Chip Heath and Dan Heath, *Switch: How to Change Things When Change Is Hard* (New York: Random House, 2010).

I thank them for their inputs and comments on some of this book's text.

Chapter 29

32. Discovery-driven planning

Rita G. McGrath and Ian C. MacMillan, "Discovery-driven Planning," *Harvard Business Review* No. 95406 (July–August 1995): 4–12.

At the outset of a new venture, too much is assumed and only a little is known. This article discusses how discovery-driven planning systematically converts assumptions into knowledge, as the venture advances.

33. Alex Andon and Jellyfish Art

Thanks to Alex Andon for sharing with me how he got into this business and how he has been sustaining that. You can find more information about Alex and Jellyfish Art on their website: www.jellyfishart.com

Chapter 33

34. Impact of culture on a firms' financial performance

Eric Flamholtz, "Corporate Culture and the Bottom Line," *European Management Journal* 19, no. 3 (2001): 268–75.

Eric Flamholtz conducted a study on the effects of corporate culture on financial performance (measured by EBIT) using regression analysis and identified a significant relationship between the two. Flamholtz is also a proponent of implementing a Culture Management Process, particularly where corporate strategy changes. The Culture Management Process entails describing the current culture, defining the desired culture, developing and implementing culture management plan, and monitor the culture.

III. Strategic Ways: Prologue

35. Small business pitfalls

Sharon Bernstein, "Small-business Pitfalls," *Los Angeles Times*, August 22, 2010.

In this article, Bernstein cited examples of entrepreneurs who started the firm without looking into all aspects of running the business.

36. Resources for entrepreneurs

Sharon Bernstein, "Resources for Entrepreneurs," *Los Angeles Times*, August 22, 2010.

Bernstein cited some useful avenues and websites for the entrepreneur to look for mentorship and support.

Chapter 37

37. Disentangle and smooth out all work assignments

John O. Whitney, op. cit.

Chapter 38

38. Consider a change in the business design

Adrian Slywotzky, *Value Migration* (Boston: Harvard Business School Press, 1995).

Slywotzky points out how firms should work on their business designs to align them with the changing priorities of the customers. His book discusses examples of firms that saw value migration coming and changed themselves. The book also brings up the three phases of migration—value inflow, stability, and value outflow.

Chapter 39

39. Creativity does not have to be artsy-creative or research- or technology-creative

Adrian Slywotzky, op. cit.

40. Starbucks selling an experience through its coffee

David Kirsch (currently with the Robert Smith School of Business), "Starbucks," *Anderson School of Management Case* (2000): 1–4.

Chapter 40

41. Mixed scanning

Amitai Etzioni, op. cit.

42. Ajay Lavakare and RMSI

Ajay Lavakare grew RMSI from a GIS and software development start-up to one of India's best employers. I have worked with Ajay and have seen some of the best practices he has incorporated at RMSI, and has brought it to its present being. Please visit the company's website at www.rmsi.com

Chapter 41

43. Basic rules of interviewing

T.J. Rodgers, op. cit.

Chapter 44

44. Three important phases in business design

Adrian Slywotzky, op. cit.

45. Presentation Zen

Garr Reynolds' Presentationzen.com is a blog site to learn some great presentation skills and pointers for putting your message across.

Chapter 45

46. Very productive and highly motivated employees

Jeffrey Pfeffer, op. cit.

Chapter 47

47. Bond due to commonality

Noah Goldstein, op. cit.

Chapter 49

48. Changing customer preferences widens the competitive playing field

Adrian Slywotzky, op. cit.

49. We take the labor out of your delivery

Ellie and Melissa, the founders of this multi-platformed company (Ellie & Melissa, The Baby Planners), guide expectant and new parents through the overwhelming and ever-changing baby product marketplace. Please visit their website (www.thebabyplanners.com) for more information on them.

Chapter 50

50. Recruitment of evangelists among customers

Guy Kawasaki, *The Art of the Start* (New York: Portfolio, 2004), 173.

According to Kawasaki, a venture should have a meaning—it should increase quality of life, right a wrong, and prevent the end of something good. He discusses how to seed the clouds and watch sales grow. Kawasaki also talks about a 10/20/30 rule for presentations, where a presentation should not exceed 10 slides, go for more than 20 minutes, and be written in a font size smaller than 30. Please visit www.alltop.com to learn about Kawasaki's latest venture.

■

About the Author

SHIL NIYOGI has helped entrepreneurial firms streamline their existing operations to drive profitability. Currently, as a member of the senior management group at a technology consulting firm in California, USA, he helps municipal governments and public agencies manage their work flows and operations better.

Shil started his career as a risk engineer right after his Civil Engineering from Delhi College of Engineering (now Delhi Technological University) in India. While still a risk engineer, he studied the emerging insurance market in India and its relevance to the Indian economy, and wrote a series of articles for the *Economic Times* in 1999. Subsequent to that, he consulted at a Big 5 firm and redesigned some of their client satisfaction tracking programs there. During that time, he also published articles on Internet Branding, explaining how virtual estate would enable brand building, particularly for entrepreneurs. He got his MBA at UCLA Anderson School, USA, specializing in entrepreneurship. At Anderson, he revived the Operations association, and also co-founded a news-journal, on new management styles and innovations, for distribution to entrepreneurs. Ever since then, he has been working with entrepreneurs and innovators helping them gather intelligence to manage operations more effectively and service customers better.